O9-BUD-339

Home ice.

PRICE: $20.00 (3798/anfarp)

DEC - - 2018

REFLECTIONS OF A
RELUCTANT HOCKEY MOM

Home
ICE

ANGIE ABDOU

ST. THOMAS PUBLIC LIBRARY

Copyright © Angie Abdou, 2018

Published by ECW Press
665 Gerrard Street East
Toronto, Ontario, Canada M4M 1Y2
416-694-3348 / info@ecwpress.com

All rights reserved. No part of this publication
may be reproduced, stored in a retrieval system,
or transmitted in any form by any process —
electronic, mechanical, photocopying, recording,
or otherwise — without the prior written
permission of the copyright owners and ECW
Press. The scanning, uploading, and distribution
of this book via the Internet or via any other
means without the permission of the publisher
is illegal and punishable by law. Please purchase
only authorized electronic editions, and do not
participate in or encourage electronic piracy
of copyrighted materials. Your support of the
author's rights is appreciated.

To the best of her abilities, the author has related
experiences, places, people, and organizations
from her memories of them. In order to protect
the privacy of others, she has, in some instances,
changed the names of certain people and details
of events and places.

Editor for the Press: Susan Renouf
Cover design: David A. Gee

LIBRARY AND ARCHIVES CANADA
CATALOGUING IN PUBLICATION

Abdou, Angie, 1969–, author
Home ice : reflections of a reluctant
hockey mom / Angie Abdou.

Issued in print and electronic formats.
ISBN 978-1-77041-445-7 (softcover).
ALSO ISSUED AS: 978-1-77305-265-6 (EPUB).
978-1-77305-266-3 (PDF)

1. Abdou, Angie, 1969– —Family.
2. Hockey for children. 3. Mother and child.
4. Hockey players—Family relationships.
5. Hockey. 6. Parenting.

I. TITLE.

GV848.6.C45A23 2018   796.962083
C2018-902557-3   C2018-902558-1

The publication of *Home Ice* has been generously supported by the Canada Council for the Arts, which last year invested $153 million to bring the arts to Canadians throughout the country. *Nous remercions le Conseil des arts du Canada de son soutien. L'an dernier, le Conseil a investi 153 millions de dollars pour mettre de l'art dans la vie des Canadiennes et des Canadiens de tout le pays.* We also acknowledge the support of the Ontario Arts Council (OAC), an agency of the Government of Ontario, which last year funded 1,737 individual artists and 1,095 organizations in 223 communities across Ontario for a total of $52.1 million, and the contribution of the Government of Ontario through the Ontario Book Publishing Tax Credit and the Ontario Media Development Corporation.

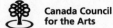

PRINTED AND BOUND IN CANADA

PRINTING: FRIESENS   5   4   3   2

"HAVE FUN! TRY HARD!"
REFLECTIONS OF A
HOCKEY MOM

"Have fun! Try hard!" That was the coach's rallying cry for every pre-Novice hockey game during my son's first year in the sport. "Have fun! Try hard!" I love it. The slogan applies to so much in life — work, writing, marriage. If you have fun and try hard, the rest often sorts itself out.

I wrote the slogan in red crayon on a torn piece of paper and taped it to the laptop where I spend my days either teaching creative writing students online or pounding out my own stories. The slogan stands as a reminder that, sure, okay, I will likely never make the writer's equivalent of the NHL and, yes, I know, I cannot expect a pot of gold at the end of the novelist's rainbow. I can, though, enjoy the process. I can take pride in my work. I can always push myself to do better. I can find meaning in the challenge. And those things — in and of themselves — can be enough. They have to be.

If hockey began and ended with that "Have fun! Try hard!" philosophy, I would have no reservations about my son's participation in the sport.

At nine years old, Oliver has already played hockey through two years of pre-Novice, one year of Novice, and his first year of Atom. Counting a previous year of skating lessons, five of his winters have been spent at the rink. Each year, the *Have fun! Try hard!* slogan feels less relevant to our experience of the game. I have arenas full of reservations.

I don't have to spell out what's wrong with hockey. There's the violence. The threat of spinal and head injuries. The parents. Especially the parents. A league on Vancouver Island has actually banned parents from attending games. The kids play before empty stands, a stroke of brilliance as far as I'm concerned. This winter in Marysville, British Columbia, at the coldest rink in North America, I saw two adults — two fathers — get in a fist fight in the stands at an Atom hockey game. Atoms are nine and ten years old. I watched these men hammer each other in the head, spitting obscenities, as mothers with babies on their hips fled to the closest change rooms to hide, and I thought, *What on earth am I doing here?*

• • •

But my reservations about hockey might run even deeper than these typical complaints about hockey violence and crazed, delusional hockey parents. I was raised in 1980s Moose Jaw, Saskatchewan. Home of the WHL Warriors.

Alarm bells are already ringing for Canadian readers. Even before I mention names like Sheldon Kennedy and Theo Fleury. Even before I mention Graham James.

Theo Fleury played for coach Graham James from the age of

thirteen, first on the Junior team, the Winnipeg Warriors. When the WHL moved the team to Moose Jaw, Fleury and James moved too. "Graham was on me once or twice a week for the next two years," Fleury writes of his coach's assaults. "An absolute nightmare every day of my life." Graham James even required Fleury to sleep at his house two nights a week rather than at the family home where he'd been billeted. Nobody questioned this arrangement. Nobody tried to put a stop to it. In 2009, more than twenty years later, Fleury published *Playing with Fire* and filed a criminal complaint against Graham James, who subsequently pled guilty to charges of sexual assault. I don't remember anyone in Moose Jaw expressing surprise.

Theo Fleury and I are nearly the same age, so his nightmare with Graham James happened while I too was a teenager in Moose Jaw. You could often find me and my gravity-defying hair at the local rink. Before games, my friends and I would shimmy into our tightest acid-wash jeans. To get them on, we'd lie flat on our backs and hook the tip of a hanger into the zipper tag, suck in our stomachs, hold our breaths, and yank. That's how we made sure our jeans fit just right. Hockey players were a big deal. It was important to look our best.

My little brother — two years younger than Theo — also played hockey. My brother, Justin, was a strong and athletic kid, physically mature for his age. Now kids can be drafted at fourteen, but back then there was no Bantam draft. Instead, each team had a protected players list of fifty, which included players of all ages. As soon as my brother turned twelve, the Warriors put him on their protected players list. He was the only Moose Jaw kid listed. The way I remember it is that when my brother turned fourteen, Graham James asked him to practice with the Warriors and play exhibition Junior games as an underage. In Moose Jaw, Saskatchewan, deals do not get bigger than this. An invitation to play Junior is a hefty step in the exact direction of the NHL. Every hockey player's dream.

The way I've always told the story, my brother said no. Even today, I can hear Justin's fourteen-year-old voice, "That Graham James guy creeps me out. No way. Keep me away from him."

I won't say everyone knew. I won't say that even in 1985 — nearly twenty-five years before the criminal charges — everyone knew. I won't say hockey culture protected Graham James, a pedophile and sex offender who used his power to prey on vulnerable boys. I won't say hockey culture victimized Theo Fleury. On those matters, I will leave readers to draw their own conclusions.

But I will say that even though I was very much on the periphery of these events — up in the stands with my impossibly big hair and my impossibly tight jeans — these events affected me more deeply than I knew.

• • •

I'd been away from the rink for decades and returning with my son felt like a kind of homecoming, though, thankfully, I'd returned wearing more comfortable pants.

My husband and I disagreed about whether to allow Ollie to play hockey. "Why would we?" my husband argued. "We live *here.*"

Here is Fernie, British Columbia. Home to a world-class ski resort with lift access just ten minutes from our house. With stunning snow-capped peaks in every direction, Fernie is a recreational dream: downhill skiing, cross-country skiing, snowshoeing, snow biking. Who would choose to get on a treacherous winter highway to spend the weekend drinking bad coffee inside a rink?

My husband had a point. My point, though, was that it is not up to us to choose. Our children's sports are like our children's marriages: we, the parents, do not get to decide. Ollie picked hockey himself. At four when he first asked to play, we put him in the figure skating club's learn-to-skate program. I got away with that

4

for two winters. Two afternoons per week he skated for an hour. We spent our weekends at the ski hill, as a family. A few months before he turned six, he told us again, "I want to play hockey." When I took him to the rink for the same learn-to-skate program, he turned his serious eyes on me. "No, Mom. I mean real hockey."

He begged us to let him play. I thought of my own childhood love for swimming, of everything that sport taught me about passion and goal setting and discipline. Any meaning I have found in life has come from those three things. Passion doesn't come from a parent saying, "We live ten minutes from a ski hill: you'll ski." Passion comes from inside. We get to have kids, but we do not get to tell them what they like.

I'm not sure I won that argument. Ollie does play hockey but I am the one braving the highways every weekend. I am the one sitting at the rink, drinking bad coffee. "As long as you love it," I tell my son. "If you love it, I'll do this. As soon as you only kind of like it, we're done. We're going skiing."

In conversation with Christian Bök, a childless poet friend, I tried to explain my devotion to my son's passion. Christian could not understand why I would sacrifice my winter (my Fernie winter) to a sport so at odds with our lifestyle. I said, "I'm sure my parents didn't want to drive me to the pool every day at five a.m."

"Oh . . ." Understanding shimmered on Christian's features. "So you're paying it forward?"

"No," I said. "I'm *parenting*."

• • •

As much as I play the martyr with my husband, Marty ("Oh, don't you worry about Ollie's hockey, I'll just do *everything*."), I do enjoy certain aspects of this return to the rink. The smell of shaved ice. Warming my hands against a cup of coffee. The magic turns of the Zamboni. And when Ollie scores a goal? His eyes find me in the stands, and he blows me a kiss.

"Did he just blow you a kiss?" the other mothers ask.

"Yes, yes, he did."

And I don't know if anything fills my heart more than the sight of my Oliver in the change room, red-cheeked and sweaty-haired, smiling ear-to-ear because he's scored a hat trick.

That's happy.

That's hockey.

Perhaps I've repressed my less sentimental memories of hockey culture.

At six, Ollie had an altercation with his coach. Ollie flips out sometimes. He can be what we like to call "challenging." I'll get to that later. For now, just imagine tears, uncontrolled rage, resolute disobedience. The coach, who'd recently been to a seminar on the importance of strict discipline, got a bit "in Ollie's face," as we say in Moose Jaw. He got a bit loud. Ollie can do loud too. It wasn't a shiny Tim Hortons hockey moment. Once we all got home, my husband sat Ollie down to explain to him the athletic code of conduct. "What the coach tells you to do, Ollie, you do it. Whatever it is, your only answer is 'Yes, coach! Yes, sir!'"

My blood turned cold. I could feel my throat closing. "Whoa! Whoa! Whoa!" At first my voice came out strangled, but I picked up volume quick enough. I'm sure the rising note of frantic alarm seemed vastly out of proportion to my husband and my son. "You do *not* say, yes, sir! You do *not* say yes to *anything* you do not *want* to do. *Not ever.*" My husband looked at me funny just in time to see me press my hand into my chest, trying to slow my galloping heart. "You do *not.*"

I hadn't thought about the Moose Jaw Warriors in decades, but suddenly Theo was there. Graham James was there. My brother — with his, "No way. That guy creeps me out. I'm not playing." — was there.

"Coaches are not always good," I added, clearly shaken. "And . . . and I don't like this game anymore. I don't . . ."

"Um, Ang, are you okay?"

6

"No. No, I am not."

So there's that little bit of ugly, festering hockey history.

But is that really what my resistance to hockey is about? We can't raise our kids under a bell jar. Bad people live everywhere. Theo Fleury had nobody looking out for him. My true reservations about hockey are perhaps a little subtler than the one panic implies.

. . .

Let me tell you about Ollie. He's "different." That's what his teachers tell me — his teachers who work in a system that is hell-bent on making kids the same. Ollie shakes his hands and chews his shirt. Dr. Google tells me both can be symptoms of autism and/or stress-anxiety disorder. Ollie has an inflexible and inflammatory sense of justice. He wants things to be right and fair. He's especially big on fairness. He wants people to be good. And fair. When he inevitably runs up against not good and not fair, he gets emotional. To this day, he has not forgiven our neighbor Crissy-C who, at two years old, right in front of Ollie in our driveway, killed a grasshopper. That happened when Ollie was *four*. Now he's nine, and the incident still brings him to tears. That dead bug and the murderous Crissy-C keep him awake at night. "That grasshopper was my friend. It might have had a family. *Why* would she do that?"

I once told my dad that reading to children increases their empathy. He responded, "I can see that, and you're creating an Ollie in a world of no more Ollies."

So, maybe it's my fault that Ollie is too sensitive for a hockey locker room.

At the start of last season (Atom Year One), the boys were charging around the dressing room in their underwear, roaring and hitting each other with their sticks (in Atom, moms are still allowed in the change rooms, since the boys can't tie their own skates). One of those boys is Quinn. I make a habit of being friendly with these boys and learning their names just to be sure they realize that I am *watching* them and I *know* who they are and they had *better* be nice to my boy. (Yes, I know, cue psychothriller background music, zoom in on the crazed mother.)

So, Quinn stomped on a spider. The boys all hollered over the impressive display of blood and guts and gore. I tried to position myself between Ollie and the scene. *Don't cry. Don't cry. Don't cry.* I tried to put the words in my expression as I met his eyes and held my hands lightly to his cheeks. *Please, Ollie. Please don't cry.*

It's not that I believe boys can't cry. It's not that I'm trying to enforce a hypermasculine code of conduct. It's not that I don't understand how harmful gender stereotypes can be. It's simply that I don't want the boys to make fun of him.

"Mom," Ollie said, his eyes already brimming, his mouth twisting the way it does just before he loses the battle with his gargantuan emotions. "WHY?" He wrung his hands. "WHY would they do that?"

"It's okay, Ollie. Let's just get your skates on." The boys were already looking our way, still in their underwear, sticks frozen overhead.

"But the spider is *dead*," Ollie said, holding himself together, though the quiver in his voice and the tears on his cheeks hinted that his composure might not last. "There's no reason to kill a living thing," he continued, "unless maybe if . . . like . . . you're going to make a steak or something . . ."

That's Ollie.

Being a human is hard. Ollie understands ethical conflict. He lives it, every day.

• • •

I fought the attempts to have Ollie diagnosed until late in grade three. I didn't want a label. He's Ollie. He has Ollie-ness. He suffers from Ollie-itis. This year, though, I decided maybe a label would help, maybe a label would come with coping strategies. We saw a counselor. I braced myself for the words she would attach to him.

"Ollie," she told me, "is what we call a highly sensitive child."

Okay.

The counselor read the symptoms: overdeveloped sense of empathy; tendency to process all the details in a room; tendency to immerse oneself in the struggle and challenges of others; tendency to get overwhelmed; extremely emotional; tendency to process situations at a very deep and complex level; inclination to escape into imagination when bored.

"*Oh no!*" I said. "He's a *writer*."

I remembered the first time Ollie — at three — recited one of his own stories to me so we could make his first book. "Don't you think it ends a little abruptly," I said, jotting down his last line. "Do you maybe want more of a gradual, full finish?"

"Mom," he said, practically rolling his three-year-old eyes, "that *is* the dénouement!"

Right. So I've got a writer. I worry about my little artist, how he will cope at the hockey rink. Will he be safe? Can he be happy there?

But here is the thing about sport. For all our *Have fun! Try hard!*, you know what makes kids happy in sports? Winning. Scoring goals. Being *good*. That's the thing I'm *not* supposed to worry about as an enlightened parent: is he any good?

Having fun and trying hard — *that's* our focus. But here's the catch: nothing is more fun than scoring goals.

Ollie's birthday is December 17th. Anyone who has heard of Malcolm Gladwell's *Outliers* knows that a December birthday for a hockey player sucks. Very early on, resources are directed toward the best kids. When kids are little, a few months can make a significant difference in development. A child who just turned five will generally not be as good as a child who is almost six, even though they are in the same age group. More resources, therefore, go to the January and February babies, and as a result those early-in-the-year children *do* become the best players. With a December birthday, Ollie is the youngest player on the ice every second year. In the words of my brother, it's not fair that a kid should have to pay for the poor planning of his parents. "You and Marty could've waited a month," says Justin, a January baby.

Ollie's first year of Atom was pretty brutal. He'd only played one year Novice (for players under nine) and hoped to stay there for a second year with his friends and grade three classmates. But he's big for his age, and the Fernie Minor Hockey Association decided it was time to go by the book and move him into Atom (for players under eleven), even if he would be only eight for nearly half the season. He didn't score a goal all year. *Not one.* I know because he tells me often. I thought this might be the year that killed it for him — the love — but in April we were playing in the waves in Mexico, and I said, "You love this! Maybe surfing is your favorite sport!"

Without hesitation, he said "Surfing is second. *Hockey* is my favorite sport."

So a year of no goals was hard, a year of being the youngest (and sometimes the worst) player on the ice was hard, but that tough season wasn't enough to kill Ollie's love for hockey or to dull its allure that I don't understand and can't control.

My brother, who played triple A hockey in Moose Jaw, was also an Olympic wrestler. After high school, he chose to go to Simon Fraser University, which competes against American schools, and he won four national championships in the National Association of Intercollegiate Athletics. In fact, during his university career, he never lost a single match to an NAIA opponent. He competed for Canada in the 2000 Olympic Games. I've watched him closely. He was good. He won almost always. He had the success that sport parents dream of for their children.

In my 2007 novel, *The Bone Cage*, I explored my worries about sport as they manifest in my brother. I know how tied up one's identity can get with success in sport. I know how all-consuming that focus on gold can be. I worry about the transition to post-sport life.

Theo Fleury wanted to be good. People told him he would never make the NHL. He was too poor. His parents had checked out. He was way too small. Being devoted and loyal and obedient to his coach — that was Theo's chance for greatness through sport. He believed that.

Obsession over sporting success can destroy lives.

Yet.

There is also something inherently hypocritical and superficial about the enlightened parents' insistence that winning doesn't matter. What does that mean exactly? Why, then, are we keeping score? Why are we even playing games in which the objective is for our team to get goals while stopping the other team from getting goals?

• • •

I have mentioned sacrificing my weekends. I have mentioned venturing out on deadly mountain highways in the worst of winter. I haven't yet mentioned the cost. In 2011, a Royal Bank survey of parents across Canada found families spend an average of $1,500 a year on hockey. Many spend much more. A 2013 American article on ESPN puts the cost higher, adding up a lifetime total of necessary purchases parents might forget to tally in the year-to-year bustle: $2,645 for skates, $1,250 for helmets, $150 for elbow pads, $180 for shin guards, $400 for gloves, $15 for Febreze spray and drier sheets, $40 for special hockey detergent, $1,750 for sticks. The article goes on to include dues and camps and travel and eventually adds up to a grand total of $48,850 U.S. for one child's experience in youth hockey. "I'm just like an ostrich in the sand,"

11

one mother wrote. "I'm sure it's $10,000 to $15,000 a season for one AAA novice son."

Do I really want to pay $15,000 a year for the privilege of driving three hours to Creston and watching my son's team get trounced 17–3? Do I want to pay that kind of money for a son who is sometimes the weakest player on the ice? For a son who is always sad because he hasn't scored a single goal all season?

In the last tournament of Ollie's first Atom season, his underdog team shockingly fought their way into the final and, oh my god, were they stoked. They were up against a big-city team — a team with bigger kids, a team with more second-year kids, a team with better kids. But you should've seen our boys play. They did not give up. The two teams were back and forth for the full three periods. We were up two goals. We were down one. Back up. Then down. We parents cheered until we were hoarse. My butt did not touch my seat once. My cheeks hurt from smiling. And Ollie! I wish you could've seen my Ollie! The kid was on a mission, a blur of speed and energy. The other parents noticed too: "What has gotten into him? Look at him go!" And god can he skate. I haven't mentioned how he skates, have I? Long, strong strides. When he makes up his mind to go, nobody can beat him. Ollie on ice: it's a thing of beauty.

He didn't get a goal that game, but he stopped the other team from getting three. In front of the net, he was a brick wall. Every time he went into a skirmish on the boards, he came out with the puck. Every time he stepped on the ice, he got credited with assists.

In the end, his team lost by one goal. Most of the kids didn't care. They were ecstatic with their silver medals. But two kids cared. One was Remy, the team's top goal-scorer. The other? Ollie. Ollie and Remy were inconsolable. From the stands, I saw the tears and the mucus, the shaking and the red face, the pounding of the stick on the ice, the accusatory glare at the refs. *Of course,* the accusatory glares at the refs. By the time the other team started throwing their gloves and sticks in the air, I was down to ice level, face to the glass. *Please. Please, Ollie. Hold it together. Please.*

Ollie does not like when a team over-celebrates. It's not nice. It is not fair.

The two teams lined up for the Player of the Game awards. We don't pay much attention to this part. In all of his years in hockey, Ollie had never been awarded Player of the Game. But he hunkered in line, his scowling face covered in snot, his shoulders heaving with sobs. I patted the glass to get his attention. *It's okay,* I mouthed. *It's just a game.* He refused to look my way. His scowl deepened.

". . . and for the Fernie Ghostriders," the coach said. "The player with the most heart, the player who tries his hardest every time he steps on the ice, the player who always busts his butt for his team. Nobody loves hockey the way this boy loves hockey. Player of the Game: number eleven *Ollie Abdou!*"

As Ollie skated back into line with his award, he found my eyes and lifted his trophy in a toast, an almost reluctant smile spreading across his snot-covered face.

The player with the most heart? Ollie is nothing but heart. And it looks like he and his big heart will be back for Atom Year Two. I will have to learn to parent an athlete in a sport that I'm not even sure I like. Together, we will try this hockey thing for another season, I've promised, as long as he *loves* it.

CHAPTER ONE

SUMMER HOCKEY CAMP
WHAT'S LOVE GOTTA
DO WITH IT?

Nothing says Canadian summer like shelling out three hundred bucks for hockey camp. Oh wait. Look whose feet have grown since April. Make that five hundred. It's August now, and I can think of many places I'd rather be than at the rink. We could be floating down the Elk River in our raft named *Fish Hunter*, or diving off the cliffs into the clear icy waters of Silver Springs, or hiking in the old-growth cedar forest. We could be white-water rafting, mountain biking, canoe camping. But we are here — in a stinking, sweaty change room — lacing up skates. Again. When I imagine a portrait of my life these days, it's that: a size six hockey skate propped between my knees, laces waiting.

Ollie has grown over the summer — not just physically — and I feel him pushing to separate from me in new ways. Sometimes he acts like there could be nothing more embarrassing than having a mother. Before we even go inside the rink, we have this conversation:

"Okay, you can come in. Just don't say *I love you, Ollie.*"

"Okay."

"And don't say: *be a good boy for your coaches, Ollie.*"

"Okay." I wait for more, but he's silent. "Can I take your picture?"

"God! Mom. No. Do *not* take my picture."

"But I can pay for your hockey camp and then stand there silently, waiting to tie your skates?" I make sure to put a hint of laughter in my voice. I want him to know that though I tease, I get where he's coming from.

"Yes, okay, you can tie my skates." Completely serious. If there's any humor in this conversation, Ollie has missed it.

"Mom? Sorry?" Ollie apologizes a lot. He's inherited my tendency to overthink, my capacity for guilt.

"It's all right, Ollie. I understand." And I really do. It is not easy becoming a big boy. And the hypermasculinity of hockey culture does not make it any easier.

Inside the arena, we parents all have the same semi-stunned expression. Our bodies move through the well-worn routines, but we do not engage our minds. If we do, we might turn and run.

I follow Ollie into the change room. I don't offer to carry any of his hockey stuff. I've learned that lesson ("Mom! I'm not three. I'm not a baby."). So I trail behind him, my hands empty, and watch him struggle with his oversized equipment bag. I want to stop us both.

Hey, Ollie, I nearly say, *how about if we just grab an ice-cream cone and go to the beach? We could bring the sand pails, catch and release some minnows.*

I doubt he would object. He loves hockey, yes, but like most nine-year-old boys, he also loves eating ice cream. It's summer holidays. Hockey camp is hard work. I wonder: have we all gotten so invested in the idea of organizing our kids' activities, of giving them every opportunity to be their best — of always "progressing the progression" as one of my less likeable fictional characters puts it — that we've forgotten how to let kids be kids?

What do we want for our children? Happy childhoods, right? Happy lives. That's all. Wouldn't they be happier at the beach?

The hockey players leaving the change room as we enter look to be about twelve or thirteen years old. Already they're big, with muscles. They smell bad. They have acne. They seem a different species than my Ollie, who still likes to cuddle, sometimes. But Ollie will be one of these gargantuan man-boys in three years. I pull a sweater over my summer clothes, bend down to find his skates, and wonder: is this really how we want to spend those three years?

A woman whose face I recognize, though I can't quite grab her name, kneels next to me and starts pulling equipment from her son's bag. She's the mom of a boy a year older than Ollie, an Ethan or a Matthew or a Jackson. "How's it going?" She doesn't look at me as she asks, and she means it as more of a salutation than a question, but I respond anyway.

"Oh. You know. It's alright. We're here. At the rink. Again."

"Only for another eight months or so," she says, laughing.

It hits me like a prison sentence. She's right. Today is the start of another eight months of hockey. I'd imagined this hockey camp as a summer visit to the rink, a brief interlude in our sandier activities. I had not thought of it as the start of a new season. But, yes, she is right. In a week, Atoms have their annual three-on-three tournament and then tryouts and then the season.

Atom Year Two has begun.

It's still thirty-two degrees outside, but hockey is ON.

• • •

I waffled a bit about summer camp. Ollie said he'd go, but he didn't say it with any enthusiasm.

17

So I did my usual check-in: "Are we done with hockey?" I've been asking this question pretty regularly since he first stepped on the ice with a stick, just to make sure. "Because if you don't want to play anymore, that's okay. Just say. You could swim or ski or some other sport."

"MOM. *You* are the swimmer. I am the hockey player."

I'm suspicious of his phrasing. It's not just about playing hockey. It's about *being* a hockey player. I've seen how this yoking of identity and sport can be destructive. "But you still like *playing* hockey, right? You think hockey is fun?"

"Of course I like playing hockey. It's my favorite sport. I *love* it."

If you love it — that's been my mantra. I tell Ollie I will pay the bills and I will sacrifice my weekends and I will brave the icy highways and I will chaperone the crazed nine-year-olds. I will put up with the cowbells and the shrieking moms and the angry dads. I will do it all — as long as Ollie loves it.

But the first time he whines or sulks, the first time he drags his butt about going to practice, the first time he complains about spending a weekend at a tournament: We. Are. Done.

The first time he only kind of likes it?

Finished.

I have made that rule perfectly clear: we do this hockey-thing only for love, and only for *his* love.

But what does that mean? To love a sport? As a recovering medievalist, I've always been fond of Aristotle's definition of love. Love draws things together. The rock loves the ground — if you drop a rock, it's drawn to the ground. A rock cannot resist the ground. That's love. Rock loves ground.

I picture Ollie rolling his eyes. *That's not love! That's gravity!*

But maybe love is a lot like gravity: a force of nature, impossible to resist, intrinsic to the workings of everything, even if we never see it. I asked my friend Steven Heighton why he loves hockey, and he emailed back:

Ah, hockey — I'll tell you what it is for me: an hour of total freedom. If I go for a run instead, I can still think about STUFF (troubling stuff). On the ice, no time. It's just hockey. I'm there. Everything moves so fast and it's a TEAM sport, so it's both interactive and competitive. There are twelve people out there moving and thinking and reacting at once, so there's a ton for the brain to process. The game demands pure Presence. A recent example: I got some upsetting news one day and could not stop thinking about it, then went out on the ice and forgot all about it for an hour. I mean, for a full hour that drunken mind-monkey shut the fuck up! Beautiful. Likewise, the day I learned I'd won a Governor General's Award, I played soon after getting that delightful phone call and, I swear, I forgot all about the news for most of the game. Either way, whether you're skating circles around gloom or ego-gratification, it's really healthy, a meditation. And speaking of meditation and the spiritual side of play, here's Krishna addressing Arjuna in the Mahabharata*: you must play as if the world hangs in the balance, but your opponent is indistinguishable from yourself.*

As a nine-year-old, Ollie can't yet articulate what draws him to hockey. I asked him if, like Steven, he finds hockey helps him forget his troubles. He answered, "Well, when I'm on the ice, I *don't* think about school." We laughed. Ollie rarely thinks about school, even when he's *at* school. After we finished laughing, I pushed him to try to explain what he loves about hockey. He stuttered out an answer that even he didn't find satisfying: "Well, I like it because it's a team game, for one . . . and I like team games, for one . . . and not to mention rough, I like rough . . . it's like being in a real-life battle scene . . . and I don't know! I just like it!"

It's unfair of me to expect him to know what drives his love for hockey. Even as an adult, I have never been strategic or rational in my love, let alone articulate. I fell for my husband for two reasons: 1) he smelled delicious, and 2) he swam a gorgeous butterfly. It was 1996 and we were teammates on the University of Western Ontario Mustangs varsity swim team.

I've since learned that such animal attraction, whether we women admit it or not, is typical. A man who smells good has an immune system opposite to that of the woman. This difference helps to ensure healthy children should the two mate.

Nature has done its job. Marty and I have two kick-ass healthy kids. Unfortunately, nature doesn't care to help us out with the more challenging aspects of marriage and parenting. Marty still has a beautiful butterfly, but he and I disagree on an awful lot when it comes to the kids.

Should we let Ollie play hockey?

I say yes. (He loves it.)

Marty says no. (We're not a hockey family.)

Do we both need to go to all of Ollie's games?

I say yes. (That would be nice; Ollie would like it.)

Marty says no. (Three of us shouldn't sit in the stands, eating poutine, while one of us exercises.)

Marty, in fact, misses most of Ollie's games, not because he's a bad parent, but because he doesn't want our daughter, seven-year-old Katie, raised as a rink rat. If we all go to the games, what will Katie do? For the most part, I agree with him, like the time a four-year-old boy (his face covered in an unfortunate combination of pop, dirt, candy, and boogers) ran out from under the bleachers and snarled at me: "Have you seen my fucking mom anywhere?"

One point Marty.

No rink rats for us. I let him take Katie elsewhere.

We have, then, approached kid sport the way most parents do: divide and conquer. Marty takes charge of Katie's ski-racing commitments, and I'm saddled with Ollie's hockey obligations. In other words, from early September until late March, my husband and I rarely see each other.

Hockey works to divide couples in this way, almost always.

Most of the children on Ollie's team have one parent in the stands, the other one off with siblings who figure skate or ski race or speed swim.

Those parents who, like Marty, argue for the benefits of skiing over hockey assert that skiing "is a family sport." The whole family can stay fit and healthy, instead of sitting in stands. Everyone can do the activity together, recreationally for now. Since I rarely see my husband from the start of fall, through the winter, and into spring, I cannot come up with a convincing rebuttal to this alleged superiority of skiing over hockey. In the place of convincing arguments, I have only one reason for forgoing the slopes to stick it out with hockey: Ollie *loves* hockey.

• • •

But I don't know that I'd say he *loves* summer hockey camp.

Our main slogan, which we've now elevated to the status of family motto, is *Have fun! Try hard!* What this motto doesn't acknowledge is that trying hard and having fun do not always go together. Sometimes, trying hard is just *hard*. Spending August afternoons doing hockey drills falls *firmly* in the *hard* camp.

I remember how hard I worked at swimming and how much the sport taught me about discipline and work ethic and commitment, and I wonder how much my job as a parent involves pushing that part of sport, the *work* part. Because given the option, Ollie might much of the time prefer to stay home and play *Minecraft* with his friends. Most kids probably would.

As he gets older, and the work part gets more intense, he is not going to love hockey all the time. Maybe he's not even going to love hockey most of the time. An athlete's connection to sport reminds me of a friend who had a challenging relationship with his girlfriend during graduate school. I lost track of how many times they broke up and got back together. When they finally decided to get married (and they're still married now, twenty years later), he told me, "We realized that though it's often hard for us to be together, it's harder for us to be apart."

Relationships are like that, right? Not always fun. One day Ollie will have to make that call about his relationship with sport: is he putting more into hockey than he gets out of it? Or is hockey still rewarding enough to account for the days he'd rather be eating ice cream at the beach, the days when training involves sacrifice and pain? Is it harder to be together or apart? That gravitational pull defines love.

• • •

Some families have already made their choice and don't have the same dilemma; maybe they easily chose the beach or slopes over the rink. There has been a clear move away from hockey in Canada. While the 570,000 players registered with Hockey Canada is an impressive number, it is down over 200,000 from its height in 2012. Unable to afford the exorbitant cost of our nation's pastime and worried about the prevalence of head injuries, parents are pulling their children from hockey and redirecting them toward soccer and swimming and other safer, cheaper sports. Even in 2013, nearly twice as many Canadian children under the age of fourteen played soccer than hockey. This is undoubtedly enhanced by the number of new Canadians whose home country is soccer obsessed. Their sports heroes are soccer stars, not hockey players. Since 2013, there have been more children playing hockey in the United States than in Canada. In the U.S., the number of hockey players increases every year. In the 2015–2016 season, USA Hockey had 542,583 players, almost exactly 100,000 more players than ten years earlier.

Many experts believe that those Canadian kids who do play hockey play too much. Hockey has become an expensive sport, with wealthy parents sending their children to elite hockey schools at increasingly young ages. Some families without the disposable income work extra jobs or go into debt to give their children the opportunity to excel at the rink. Malcolm Gladwell's claim that being good at anything takes 10,000 hours struck a chord with this overachieving parental group, and they want their kids to be good. Concussions are only one downside to this excess. The increased ice time takes a severe toll on the body, particularly on growing joints. Sport-medicine experts warn that hockey culture is producing future candidates for arthritis and hip replacements.

There's also fatigue. Simply put, even the best kids (especially the best kids) are getting sick of hockey well before they reach Gladwell's magic 10,000 hours. Since 2009, players in the upper age groups (Pee Wee, Bantam, and Midget) have declined 7.4 percent. Many talented hockey players burn out by the time they reach thirteen.

Raised in an athletic family, I am susceptible to the *more more more* approach to sport. The Olympic motto, after all, is *Faster! Higher! Stronger!* It's not *Have fun! Be fair! Learn life lessons!*

Knowing that I am capable of this mindless drive to push myself in the name of improved athletic performance — and knowing that one of the main things I got from that drive is arthritic shoulders — I plan to check in with myself as a parent and stay aware of that point at which hockey crosses over from play into something far less healthy.

• • •

In response to this check-in, we have already scaled back Ollie's hockey participation. His school offers a program called Hockey Academy where students can get out of class two mornings a week to practice hockey skills. Because I do love to complain about how much money I spend on hockey, let me say: Hockey Academy is expensive. Nine hundred dollars of expensive. Ollie did Hockey Academy from grade one through grade three. Partly, I thought he'd find it fun to get out of school for ice time. Partly, I wanted to give him an advantage to counteract his late birthday. My

23

dad (also a proponent of the *Faster! Higher! Stronger!* approach to sport) told me that the skill-based work at Hockey Academy would be the best thing for Ollie's game.

At first, Ollie liked Hockey Academy. It appealed to that identity part of sport: knowing where he belongs, having his people, feeling special. Still last year, when I showed up to the classroom to drive the three players to the rink — "Hockey boys! It's time to go!" — they lit up, bounding toward me and out the door while the rest of their classmates slumped over their math sheets. The teacher excused the "hockey boys" from math. That passes for high status in a grade-three kid's world.

Sometimes, we parents cling to the notion of ourselves doing what's best for our kids. That was me. "I've paid my nine hundred dollars! I'm taking time out of my work day to shuttle kids to the rink! My son is getting valuable skills training! Hockey instead of math? Lucky boy!"

Caught up in my own super-mom back patting, I didn't pay as much attention as I should have when Ollie's enthusiasm faded at that call of "Hockey boys!"

Ollie does not like change. I see now how leaving the classroom in the middle of one school activity and coming back partway through another caused him anxiety. Grade three was a bad year to begin with. His class was too big. There were too many challenging students (himself sometimes included). His teacher was overwhelmed. He absorbed her emotions, the way my empathetic kid does. He also found the chaos of the room taxing. My little eight-year-old boy was totally overwhelmed and stressed out. Hockey Academy did nothing to help. I took too long to notice.

Sadly, I needed a full-fledged crisis to reconsider Ollie's participation in Hockey Academy. In February of grade three, in his first year of Atom, he had a particularly bad practice (though looking back, good Hockey Academy practices had been rare throughout the whole season). This time he was struggling with a puck-handling drill. He does not have great dexterity. Fine-motor skill activities, like tying shoes or printing neatly, have challenged him. On this very bad day, he grew frustrated at his inability to complete the assigned task (don't ask me exactly what it was: something to do with pylons, a puck, and a stick). The more frustrated he got, the more impossible the task became. The coach interpreted Ollie's inability as insubordination and continued to yell instructions at him, ones Ollie could not execute. Even as an adult, I would find someone yelling at me about something that I could not do unpleasant and stressful. Ollie got red in the face. He got snotty. He started to cry. Finally, the coach shot Ollie's puck down the ice. "Go get it!"

The coach later told me he thought Ollie needed the time to cool down.

That's not how Ollie saw it. That puck was *Ollie's* puck. The coach shooting it down the ice was not fair. The coach getting mad at Ollie when he'd tried his best was not nice. Nothing bothers Ollie more than not fair and not nice. On top of the frustrating drill, the injustice of the coach stealing his puck was too much. Ollie has never been one to take his emotions out on others — he's not a fighter or a bully — but he does sometimes take those bad feelings out on himself. This time, he skated head-first, full speed into the boards.

He could have broken his neck.

That was the end of our time in Hockey Academy.

I blamed the coach at first. His lack of insight into the situation. His misunderstanding of Ollie's motives. Maybe I'm a typical mother that way: slow to find fault in my own children. Now I wonder, what if that whole thing — that whole head-smashing thing — was simply a result of Ollie being too stressed, under too much pressure? Already. In grade three. What if his meltdown was simply a symptom of us — of *me* — asking a young boy to do too much?

We focused on finishing out grade three in a calm manner. I dropped it with the *more more more*. I reined in the notions of "giving him every opportunity to be his best." Regular Atom hockey — two evening practices per week and a game or three on the weekends — would be enough.

Enough.

There's a word you don't hear too often in sport.

But I am not thinking about any of this at summer hockey camp that leads into Atom Year Two, not really. We've had a good summer. Ollie has kept his emotions well under control. He hasn't attempted to break his own neck, not even once. We're good.

• • •

I'm not worried about him at all as I sit in the stands, watching five days of hockey camp. What I *am* worried about is how I'm going to write this book. Because here's the truth: hockey practice is boring. They shoot at that net, over and over, and then they skate forward around those pylons, over and over, and then they skate backward around that circle, over and over. And then they do it again. And then again. And then again. More than anything, sport involves repetition. The great sport movies focus on the intense drama of victory and defeat, not on the daily mundane realities of practice. With notebook in hand, I watch these little athletes do the same thing, for days, and I don't write a word.

As the week wears on, I also worry about my marriage. I'm getting mad. Marty hasn't come to the rink once. The 2016 Olympics have — as the Olympics always do — made him a slave to the television. He's particularly obsessed with the unprecedented success of the Canadian women's swim team, including sixteen-year-old sprinting sensation Penny Oleksiak. By the end of the Games, Oleksiak will have won more medals than any Canadian woman swimmer in a single Olympics. In fact, she will have won more medals than *any* Canadian athlete in *any* sport in *any* Olympic Games ever. Announcers keep exclaiming that all this success has come despite Penny's late start in the sport. At nine, she decided she wanted to become a competitive swimmer and her parents signed her up for a year of private lessons to catch up. At ten, she joined her first speed swimming team. Throughout the Games, sportcasters repeatedly cite this start as evidence that athletes don't have to pick their sport at too young of an age.

Is nine years old really a *late* start in sport? By that criteria, Ollie should have picked his sport by now and little Katie is fast running out of time. I don't find the announcers' glee at Penny's "refreshingly late start" particularly encouraging. That competitive part of me — the one I try to repress — panics that I'm a bad parent because I've failed to connect my little athletes to their right sport in time.

Some parents have started to push back against this panic. In a 2014 *New York Times* article called "There's No Off in this Season," Bruce Feiler, author of *The Secrets of Happy Families*, argues that *Friday Night Lights* is now Every Night Lights, and something as simple as planning a family vacation has become impossible. The more we try to keep up with the Joneses in terms of preparing our little athletes for future success, the less likely we are to leave ourselves time to enjoy the simple pleasures of family life. Feiler cites Dr. White, a pastor in North Carolina, who claims the problem is rooted in the social anxiety of contemporary parents. "Parents are so insecure, they feel like whatever other parents are doing, they have to do," he said. "If it's soccer, then my kid has to play soccer. We have elevated sports into a cultural religion. The fact that it clashes with family life is not surprising." Even now, when my oldest son is only nine years old, I can already relate to both this anxiety and this failure to maintain a well-balanced family life. I take solace in the new research, which stresses that parents do not, in fact, "create" successful athletes. I wonder if this knowledge might one day sink in enough that I could skip summer hockey camp without feeling I have failed.

On day three of summer camp, Marty tears his gaze away

from the young women swimming on television long enough to say, "I'm curious to know how Ollie's liking hockey camp."

Right. But not curious enough to come.

I don't say it aloud. From the beginning, I've known our deal with hockey. I'm the one who said yes to hockey. I'm the one responsible.

My parents don't come either. In the summer months, they live in a suite in our house. They're both retired. They're not busy. They like sports. My dad competed in hockey, wrestling, football, and squash. He won national championships in two of the four. My mom is an excellent swimmer, a record-breaking breaststroker.

I suspect they would all come if Ollie were a better player. If he happened to be the star, they'd all be sitting in the stands, watching proudly. But the camp is for Atom Year Two and PeeWee Year One. Again, Ollie is the youngest player on the ice. He struggles with coordination. He often seems a step behind.

My family's lack of interest digs at some of my own festering athletic wounds.

"They'll probably come to your game on Saturday," I tell Ollie.

He nods stoically. Everyone loves an audience. Ollie has only me.

In my youth, my brother was the star athlete, and I took the back-up role of cheering fan. My dad rarely came to my swim meets, for the same reason that I suspect he shows little interest in Ollie's hockey: I was never a star. My dad's presence was so rare at my sporting events that when he did show up, I blundered under the pressure. Once he came to my high-school basketball game, and almost as soon as I saw him sit in the stands, I ran to the wrong end of the court, waving my arms wildly and yelling for the ball, standing under the wrong net. By the time I realized my mistake, everybody had turned to look at me. *Everybody.* The fans, the cheerleaders, my team, the other team, the coaches. Finally clueing into my own idiocy, long after everyone else, I dropped my hands to my side and shuffled my red-faced self back to the action at the other end of the court.

I became what my father saw: an uncoordinated, unsuccessful, poor athlete; an unimpressive sister to a much-loved sport star; an athletic embarrassment. Even now — with fifty in my sights — fear of failure and a craving for external affirmation drive me far more than they should. Raised in the temple of competitive sport, I too often see the world in terms of winners and losers. I have some un-schooling work to do on myself. To protect my children from this tendency to overemphasize that winning/losing dichotomy, I'll need to un-teach myself soon.

I remember my best-ever swim race. I was in my mid-teens and competing in a 1500 meter freestyle at a national youth competition. Even at that young age, I must have known my main problem in sport was lack of confidence because behind the blocks that day, I decided to pretend I was my brother. *I am Justin Abdou. I can do this.* I had put in the countless hours of hard, hard work (two hours in the pool before school every morning, two more hours after). I had the training. I had the ability. I lacked the belief in myself. My confidence let me down at competitions, always. People called me "a practice swimmer," one who seems unable to rise to the occasion of competition, one who does her best swimming during training. That day, I decided to find the confidence that I needed to be a competition swimmer.

I am Justin Abdou.

I can do this.

In that 1500 meter free, *pretending* to be strong and confident and unbeatable, pretending to be my brother, I won my heat by half a length and I set a club record. The record stood for over a decade.

I never want my son to have that feeling. I never want him to think that simply being Ollie isn't good enough.

So I'll be his enthusiastic audience, even when it means sitting in an ice rink for a week in August. I'll have confidence in him even when he does not have it in himself. I will wear that confidence in my eyes so he sees it every time he looks at me, sees it so often he can't help but believe in it.

By the time the camp's final game rolls around, the Olympic swimming events have drawn to a close and Marty has extricated himself from the television room. He's making soup that involves peeling chickpeas. He stands before two piles of them, peeling one tiny chickpea at a time.

"You do not need to peel the chickpeas." I'm irritated with how quickly he's turned his attention from Penny Oleksiak to this make-work project. I suspect the new diversion will also keep him from the rink.

"The recipe says peel the chickpeas."

"Trust me: the soup will be fine with the chickpeas unpeeled."

"The instructions say *clearly*," Marty says as he flicks a slimy skin into the discard pile, "one must peel the chickpeas."

"Are you coming to Ollie's game today?" I try to keep the judgment from my voice, sort of.

• • •

Marty stays home with his garbanzo beans, but my mom and dad do finally come to the game. Within minutes of Ollie stepping on the ice, I wish they hadn't. I want them to say only that he's great. I want them to praise his effort, his enthusiasm, his improvement. I want them to beam: *isn't he cute!*

But they're athletes, and they watch sport with the same critical eyes that watched me.

"He's not anticipating," my dad says. "You've gotta see the play before it happens."

"He's holding his stick wrong."

"He's not even touching the puck."

"This is a really low level of hockey."

Every one of my dad's comments makes me feel like that

teenage girl who has just realized that she's waving her arms at the wrong end of the court. I wish he'd leave.

After my parents do leave, the coaches open the ice to a free-for-all. Both benches clear, all the kids mobbing the puck. Ollie comes to life. He charges in. He's thinking less. He's a tough and robust boy and he responds well to the more physical play. He *loves* it. In his face now, I see that love that I've been searching for all week. When he doesn't overthink the rules and all the restrictions involved in playing his position properly, he goes hard for the puck. He doesn't stress. He's in the play. I wish my dad could've seen this Ollie, and I'm embarrassed how badly I want my father's approval, even still, even for my son.

In the locker room, Ollie vibrates with excitement. Sweat flies as he pulls off his helmet. "Did you see me get that guy?"

I can't help mirroring his smile with my own. I forget all about my disappointments. But he doesn't give me a chance to respond.

"And then he got me and I got down but I got right back up and then there was me against *two* big guys . . ." The words come at me so fast that I feel I'm in the scrimmage, spinning with all those little warriors. "And then I got the puck off one them and he hip-checked me a bit but I didn't even fall over and . . ."

If I were to look up *glee* in the dictionary, there would be a picture of Ollie right now. Pure happy energy.

By the time we get to the car, though, the fatigue sinks in and Ollie quiets to a silence, resting his head against the backseat window. I admire him in the rearview mirror, his too-long hair wet with sweat, his skin glowing with exertion. *God, I love this kid.* "Good job today, Ollie."

"I didn't get any goals. I never get any goals." He holds his hand out the window, opening and closing his fingers against the wind.

"But you had fun."

"Yeah." It's a weak yeah. I'm not sure why I can't let the down moment sit, but I need to pull back the post-battle Ollie, victorious in the change room. Even if the victory existed only in his own imagination.

"You tried really hard. I know sport is a lot of work now that you're older. And I know it's your summer holidays. I'm proud of you for trying so hard, Ollie."

"Mom?"

"Yes?"

"Can you call me Oliver? Ollie . . . it's more of a baby name."

"Okay."

We'd planned the short-form to long-form switch when we first named him, giving him a young, cute nickname and a more mature name to grow into. I picture him then in his hospital-issued yellow jumper, his tiny foot pulled free, still black from the midwife inking it to make a print. The moment is so close I can smell it. It brings back the heat of my fresh anger at the midwife who dirtied my perfect baby and made him cry. I didn't care about the print. I also remember the nurses marveling at how early our baby boy held up his own head — "Just a newborn!" — and how proud Marty and I were at this confirmation of what we already knew: this baby was a miracle. *Ollie.*

Oliver. Life, it moves so fast. Just when I start to understand my boy, he grows into someone new. An Oliver. "Sure," I answer again. "I'll call you Oliver."

He nods, one quick movement, without turning his eyes from the window. "Mom? You don't have to get mad. This is just a yes or no question."

"Okay . . ."

"Actually, no. Never mind. It's nothing."

"Tell me."

"Well . . ." He sounds worried. He doesn't think I will like what he has to say.

I dread the teenage years when this kind of hesitance will be cause for concern. But now I can say easily and lightly, "It's okay. Really. Whatever it is. Just tell me."

"Well, Mom, do I *have* to go to hockey camp again next summer?"

Oh. God, this parenting thing. Who put me in charge? Am I the only parent who feels like a fraud when confronted with such questions? When granted such authority?

I don't know. Does he have to go to summer hockey camp? If he wants to advance in any sport, yes, he will have to work very hard, even in August, to get better. *Try hard! Have fun!* Hard will always be part of sport. But what if he doesn't care about advancing in sport? What if he only wants to *play* sport? Isn't that okay too? When does how much effort he wants to put into hockey become his decision, and only his decision?

My dad frequently talks about young Theo Fleury's passion for the sport. "You could tell he was going to be good because, god, he *loved* it. First player on the ice. Last player off. He'd do drills by himself for hours." Nobody could *make* Theo love a sport like that. Passion like that comes from inside, not from a parent's rules. For a moment, I'm grateful for the knowledge that creating passion does not fall within a mother's power. Parents do not create athletes. But then I remember that Georges Laraque, in *The Story of NHL's Unlikeliest Tough Guy*, claims he chose to live with his near-abusive father over his kind, nurturing mother because even as a child Georges knew his father's pressure would help him be successful in sport. Georges Laraque believes he would not have had his success in sport under the parenting of his softer, more loving mother.

Ollie waits. For now, I am the only one who can answer this question about how hard and how often my young athlete has to skate, but how am I supposed to know? I want to confess to him that I'm play-acting at adult. Inside, I'm still that bewildered teenager standing under the wrong basket and calling for the ball.

What I want is for him to *want* to go to summer hockey camp. But I want a lot of things. I want my husband to stop peeling chickpeas and come to his son's hockey games. I want to alter the way my parents see their grandson on the ice. I remember the pride I took in my work ethic during my swimming years, and I want my boy to feel the same way about work. I want my little hockey player to love the hockey camp that cost us both a week of August. I want that love to draw him toward the commitment and hard work that lead to success.

None of these things fall within my control.

As a mother, I'm here to walk with Ollie — I mean Oliver — as he builds his own life. I'm not here to build that life for him. He'll figure out his own relationship to hockey, to sport. The way he shapes that relationship will ultimately say a lot about his attitude to life's biggest issues: work, love, commitment. I have very little control over any of that. I remember the research: *parents do not create athletes.* Repeat it with me. *Parents do not create athletes.*

"No, Oliver," I finally answer, relaxing into the fresh salty smell of little boy sweat. "You don't have to go to hockey camp if you don't want to." I let that hang in the air for a while and am surprised how obvious it seems, how simple. "It's up to you, Oliver. Totally up to you."

He stays staring out the window but gives one hard quick nod of acknowledgment. "Mom?" He stops drawing on the window and leans forward so I can't see him in my mirror anymore, but then I feel him against me, his hand on my arm, his sweaty head on my shoulder. "Thanks. I love you."

"I love you more."

And for that moment, I stop worrying about my job as a sport parent and whether or not I'm doing it right. I keep my eyes on the road and squeeze his hand. He has strong, meaty paws like my brother and my dad, and his skin still feels hot to my touch. Instead of squirming away after a moment of affection, he lets me hold his hand. I will hang on to that beefy little hand for as long as he allows, and I will think only about *this* kind of love and commitment. The easy kind. The best kind.

CHAPTER TWO

GRAHAM JAMES
WHERE WERE THE PARENTS?

I've told myself a story about my brother Justin and hockey coach Graham James. My story goes like this: my brother brushed shoulders with Graham James but never encountered the abuse experienced by others. There is only enough of a connection to let me dip a toe into the Graham James conversation: "I knew him! He wanted my brother to play for him!"

In my story, my brother sidestepped any true ugliness. In my story, my brother saw James for what he was and knew enough to steer clear.

This story has a subtext. It works to assure me that my family somehow remains safe from the evil personified by Graham James. The subtext implies that the sort of horror inflicted on Theo Fleury and the other players under James's charge happens to people different from us, people less alert, less strong, less judicious than we Abdous.

This story, of course, is a fantasy. A wish.

Justin sits here with me now, drinking beer at the bonfire in my backyard. Only my brother's hands can make a can of beer look so small. Dollhouse beer. It's no surprise when he reaches for a second before I've cracked my first.

I adore my brother. My "little brother," I call him, but the label has always been ironic. Though Justin is eighteen months younger than I am, I don't remember a time he was smaller. He wrestled his way to the 2000 Olympics in Sydney by always being the strongest, the toughest, the best, and not only in his own age group. As a boy, he often won national competitions while wrestling an age category up, sometimes two. Shortly after breaking his collarbone, he competed in his own age-group national championship and placed first in Canada with his arm taped at the elbow, tight to his torso. *My brother could beat you with one arm tied behind his back.* Really. It's no wonder he was the hero of my youth.

Though we do live in the same province, we rarely see each other. He works as head wrestling coach at Simon Fraser University, always driving a van full of varsity wrestlers around the continent. Or flying with the national team to countries I will never visit (Uzbekistan, Mongolia, Iran). It's been many years since I've kept track of his schedule. On any given day, I couldn't tell you what continent he's on. But today he's in my backyard, sitting at the bonfire, tiny little beer in his gargantuan paw resting on his oversized knee. Having him to myself is a rare luxury. His presence makes me happy.

But I'm also nervous. I need to take advantage of the rare opportunity to talk to him face-to-face. I crack my beer, sip, and try to think of a way to broach this hockey book. Justin has reason to be leery of me writing about sports. When I write on athletic topics, I'm always, at least a little bit, writing about him. When I published *The Bone Cage,* a novel about the dangers of an identity being too closely tied to sporting success and the challenges of adapting to regular life after the Olympics, I held off sending him a copy of the work-in-progress as long as I could.

The week before the book went to page proofs, Marty finally told me, "Ang. You have to send it to him. What are you going to do? Let him buy it off the shelves? He's going to read it."

Still I waited, terrified that Justin would recognize himself in the book's Olympic wrestler named Digger. I worried both that Justin wouldn't like what he saw and that he would demand to know what right I had to use his life as fodder for my fiction. I don't have an answer to that question. I doubt Justin would be satisfied by me shrugging and saying, *I write what I write*. I would feel equally irked if someone took the liberty of painting me — or even parts of me — on the page. Because it would be *their view* of me, not my own, and the flesh and blood truth of me would warp in the transition from life to words. In the telling, I would solidify into the author's version of me. The malleability of real life and real people can get lost on the page.

"Of course, I borrowed the minutia of real life, to make the story believable," I told Justin before I committed *The Bone Cage* to Purolator. "I teased out themes based on ideas I've developed from the experience of those closest to me. But the novel's wrestler is mainly a product of my imagination. You might recognize shades of yourself, and that could be a bit uncomfortable, but remember as you read: Digger is fiction. Completely made up."

I talk too much when I'm nervous.

After Justin read the book, he had two comments.

His first point: "I need to teach you how to do a gut wrench. That might look like what we're doing, but in sports, more happens than what a spectator sees. It'd be like thinking everything anyone needs to know about swimming happens above the water."

I imagined myself down on the ground, face grinding into the carpet, while Justin squeezed the last ounce of air out of me, and I did not look forward to him "showing me how to do a gut wrench." I suggested he demonstrate on Marty instead.

Justin's second point hit closer to my fears about the book: "You were right. I *did* recognize myself in Digger, and it *was* a bit uncomfortable, like you said. Kind of the way it's uncomfortable when I watch myself on television."

So. Maybe I borrowed more than a little. But my brother let me publish the book. He's even been supportive of it. We did a CBC Radio show together about what coaches can do to help their athletes manage the transition to post-Olympic life. I have no specific reason, then, to think that my brother will hate that I'm writing another sport book, but still my intuition tells me he might have had enough of me and my sport expertise.

"I just signed a contract for a new book," I venture. I want to tell him while we have the fire to ourselves. Marty will join us soon, and then my parents. "It's about hockey."

"*You* are writing a book about hockey?" Justin doesn't have to say anything more. My confidence wavers.

"Well, it's more about *parenting* hockey players. About parenting athletes, really. About the challenges of hockey culture, the complexities of navigating that line between supporting and pushing —"

"*You* are writing a *parenting* book?"

"Shut up."

My brother looks like Ollie. (Oliver has returned to Ollie. He experiments with his identity, trying on names the way teenagers switch clothes: goth, prep, jock, rocker, hipster. I'm glad, for now, to have Ollie back.) Justin and Ollie have the same thick coarse hair, the same big-toothed smile, the same light in the eyes when activities get a little rough, the same inability to lie. When they try to pass off a fib, they wear identical expressions, a slippery smirk that threatens to slide into a full laugh. Neither can tell me the slightest untruth. I like this quality. When Ollie tries, I stop him with "Whatever you're going to say, don't say it. Look at your face. You are your uncle Justin."

But this evening in my backyard, it's my brother who wears my son's face. Justin's silence implies he has nothing else to say on the matter of my forthcoming sport book. From his face, I know he lies. He has all kinds of things to say.

I change the subject. "How was Saskatchewan?" Justin had recently been inducted into the new sport hall of fame in Moose Jaw.

I watch him in the firelight as he explains that his old friend Dave Danchilla dissuaded him from using his "Graham James material" at the induction. Justin is a very funny guy, with secret stand-up comedy ambitions. He's no longer in the ring, but he still loves an audience. It's a family trait.

Sometimes Justin's performance treads the line between hilarious and offensive. I do not want to imagine his "Graham James material."

Three years earlier, before a big speaking event, Dave told Justin, "Moose Jaw is not ready for your Graham James stories." At the hall of fame induction, Justin asked Dave again — is Moose Jaw ready now? "This town," Dave said, "will never be ready for that discussion."

"Well, actually . . ." I seize the chance to bring the conversation back round to my hypothetical book. "In June, I gave a talk about hockey to my international Sport Literature Association." In the dim light, I'm not positive, but I think Justin rolls his eyes. I do hear a low *hmph* of dismissal — that I know for sure. My words pick up speed. "I talked about your experience with Graham James. The audience seemed very ready to have that conversation."

"Yeah?" Justin wears an Ollie-like smirk again, but not the one that means he's lying. I don't quite recognize this look. "You talked about me and Graham James? And your audience liked it? I bet your story wasn't about Graham James wanting to have me for one of his little sleepovers? Or how he wanted to be my special friend?"

"WHAT?" Shock makes me speak too loudly. I have held onto my version of the story for over thirty years.

Now my brother tells me . . .

I don't know: what exactly is my brother telling me?

I lower my voice. "*My* story is that Graham James wanted you to play for him and you said, 'No way. That guy creeps me out.' That's the start and the end of *my* story."

"No, no, no." Justin smiles. He finds this funny? I think of Kurt Vonnegut's designation of crying and laughing as essentially the same response. When we don't know what else to do, we cry or we laugh.

Justin would never cry.

"I *did* say James creeps me out," he explains, "but we're talking the WHL. I was fourteen. Of course I played. I played on the Warriors triple A team. I practiced with the Junior team, played some exhibition games with them. We always knew James put me on teams that I wasn't good enough for. But I still played. How could I not? I was on the Warriors' protected list as soon as I turned twelve. Then when I was sixteen, I was playing Midget triple A and James was the GM. Sheldon Kennedy was our captain. James called me into his office after practice. I'd already half undressed. I was wearing hockey pants, bare feet, no shirt. As he talked to me — just the usual hockey stuff, work harder at this, give that a try — he started taking off his clothes and just kept talking. Before I could get my mind around what was going on, he'd gotten down to his underwear. Then he sat on the arm of my chair. I pushed him to the floor and told him to stay the fuck off of me. The next day, I got traded to Medicine Hat and then to Brandon, the end of my strong march to the NHL." Justin held his position on the Warriors' protected list from the day he turned twelve until the day Graham James took off his clothes.

I don't know what to say. Graham James got nearly naked

and forced himself onto my teenage brother's chair? My little brother. What do we call that? Do we say James *sexually assaulted* my brother? According to Canadian law, a person commits sexual assault when he intentionally applies force to a person, directly or indirectly, or when he, by act or gesture, attempts to apply force, especially if he has, or causes the person to believe on reasonable grounds that he has, the ability to effect his purpose.

Maybe we could, all these years later, say James assaulted my brother. Nobody invited a nearly naked Coach James into that chair. James had authority in the situation. He violated trust. James exerted his power in a way parents like to assume coaches will not.

Let's revise my history then: my heroic brother — who brings to mind my own son in a way I suddenly find very uncomfortable — was never immune from this particular personification of evil. My brother sometimes played for Graham James. Graham James took off his clothes and approached my brother.

"You never told anyone?" Who would Justin have told? *How* would he have told it?

It has taken him thirty-two years to tell me, his only sibling, his adoring big sister.

• • •

The next day, after Justin leaves, I ask my dad about Graham James. We're on the edge of my property, at the fire pit near the forest again, but this time in broad daylight with coffee.

"Did you all know about James? What he was up to?"

"No, we didn't know."

"But were you surprised?" I'm referring to James's abuse of Theo Fleury, but I don't have to say. Anyone from Moose Jaw knows exactly what I mean. That bit of sporting history has seared itself into our brains, permanently and painfully.

"No, we weren't surprised," my dad answers, a little too quickly.

I wait, hoping he has more to say, thinking if I leave enough silence he will feel obligated to fill it. My dad looks like Justin too. The same piercing blue eyes. The same love of an audience. "I asked Graham James about your brother back then," my dad finally continues. "I said, 'What's Justin doing out there? He's only fourteen. A boy. He's never even played hit hockey before and now he's out there with adults? Those twenty-year-old men are throwing him all over the place.' You know what Graham James said? He said, 'Yeah, but just look at the way he gets back up.'"

I say nothing.

Look at the way he gets back up?

My mothering heart does not know how to respond to that.

"Graham James was a weird guy." There's a conclusive clunk to my dad's words. "Yes, everyone knew he was weird."

Winnipeg friends who had Graham James as a high school teacher use the same word: *weird.* "We were fourteen years old and he lent us his car. We drove it to the liquor store. It was weird."

So everyone, including my parents, knew Graham James was "weird." I trust everyone who uses the word "weird" also recognizes it as a euphemism, in this case quite a harmful euphemism, one that allowed too many people to look away.

My parents saw James's "weirdness," but still my parents let my brother play for him. I think about the Theo Fleury and Graham James story, and I wonder: where were the adults? Where were the parents? Where were *my* parents? Could it happen today?

• • •

To the "where were the parents" question, my own kids would likely answer, "Gone running." I've been bored over the summer. Existentially bored. I'm simply worn down by the routine of parenting, despairing at basic tasks like laundry.

Only empathetic Ollie picks up on my mood. "Are you okay, Mom? Are you okay, Mom? Are you okay?"

No, Oliver, I'm not okay.

I'm forty-seven years old. My life has fallen to the predictable. I spend more time than I'd like picking up dishes, managing sporting schedules, driving laps to and from the arena. What did I expect middle-age parenting would be like?

I cannot let my predictable midlife crisis stress out my sensitive boy. I need to right myself; like any good English major, I go to books to find answers. Sigmund Freud tells me that to be happy we need love and work: "Love and work are the cornerstones of our happiness." I know the truth of that: without work, life can seem meaningless. Goals — whether we achieve them or not — give life a narrative structure, forward movement, energy. The process of working toward goals infuses meaning into routine and repetition. Sport has always worked like that for me, rooting me and giving me a sense of purpose. Sport goals, like any work goals, create the illusion of forward movement and the excitement of (potential) victory. That momentum makes days — and lives — feel meaningful. I hope sport will work in this way for my children too, as an antidote to ennui and depression. Well managed, sport can do that. But it does take managing.

In June, I signed up for a fall half marathon, hoping the goal would re-energize me. As I scribbled out the training schedules, increased my mileage, worked out diet plans, and watched my pace times get faster, I did find a new sense of enthusiasm. But those hours I spend out running trails are hours I'm not keeping watch on my kids.

We all have our own means of looking away. Am I any different from those parents who put Graham James in a position of power over their children and then took no note of how badly he abused that power?

These are the questions that take me into Labor Day weekend. Not exactly a celebratory frame of mind to carry into the last burst of summer, a chance to do something outdoorsy and fun and memorable with the family before we return to the routines and demands of regular work-school life.

Marty tells me we should venture out and see if we can catch the final bit of a meteor shower in full darkness. "I've got the perfect spot picked in the provincial campground. No vehicle access. Hardly anyone knows about it. We'll hike in. The kids are big enough to carry in their own little backpacks. We can let them stay up late. It'll be an adventure."

"Ollie has a hockey tournament," says me, the keeper of schedules, the killer of joy. "I've got a long training run."

"On Labor Day weekend?" He's incredulous. "A *hockey* tournament?"

His tone implies that surely this time I must have my dates wrong. What kind of monster would force kids to be inside an arena on the last weekend of summer holidays?

"Yep," I assure him. "*Each year* on Labor Day weekend, Ollie has a hockey tournament. It's the local three-on-three tournament, which falls every single September exactly on Labor Day weekend." I repeat myself, enunciating each syllable. I'm annoyed. Why do I have to be the one to remember the schedule? Why do I have to be the fun-suck?

"Meteor showers. Camping. Family time. Summer. Ollie could miss hockey." Marty puts an edge in his voice to match mine. We don't have these conversations easily. I tense against a dangerous undercurrent of anger and resentment. I don't even know for sure what we're fighting about, and I wonder if other families navigate this terrain more gracefully. They must.

Neither Marty nor I ever devoted ourselves to a team game. We both focused primarily on swimming, the loneliest of sports. We're very different kinds of swimmers though. I'm a work horse. I put my head down and suffer. The more suffering involved, the more I excel. I don't always do things the prettiest way, but I muscle through. Marty, on the other hand, is a perfectionist. For him, swimming is an art, all about finesse. He believes there's one right way to do things: his way. I'm less interested in "the right way," but I'm very good at dedicating myself to hard labor and tolerating pain. We don't work well together. We could learn something from hockey. A team sport could have taught us how to take advantage of our different approaches and our different strengths, as well as the way those differences complement each other. With some practice, we might even be able to arrive at a winning strategy. But we both prefer individual sports.

"He can't miss hockey," I say. "I've paid for hockey. He's committed to a team. Hockey is a go."

"Fine. Katie and I will hike in and watch the stars. Katie and I will camp."

"Fine."

Fine. Except Katie doesn't want to go with Marty. Between hockey games, our house and backyard fill with boys playing tag and hide-and-seek and capture the flag. At seven, Katie loves boys and wants to be a part of their rough, sweaty play.

Before I had kids, I thought I wanted the house where all the children came to hang out. That way I could keep an eye on things. Now I have that house and it's great . . . except the part where *all the kids have come to hang out*! Early today, playing hide-and-seek, Katie poked her head into my room and yelled over her shoulder, "Nobody's hiding in here except my mom!"

Truth. I kicked them all outdoors, asked the neighbor to keep an eye on them, and took myself out for a run.

Now I'm stretching in the living room to the soundtrack of shrieks and giggles. One day I will miss this. Between quad and hamstring stretches, I wander out to the back deck, keeping watch over the wild outdoor activities.

Katie has always been an independent girl. Her first full sentence was "I do it."

"I'll feed you."

"I do it."

"Let me help you with your jacket."

"I do it."

"I'm going to wash your hair."

"I do it."

She's the opposite of Ollie, and I don't feel the same need to hover and protect. I watch Katie more for the sheer entertainment.

She enjoys roughhousing with all the big boys, but today she sticks especially close to Ollie's friend Dylan. He's a fast, agile kid and a great athlete, but small. Though he's two years older than Katie, she stands at least as tall as he does.

Today's game involves a lot of running between the woods and the garden shed. I love watching Katie, her limbs long, her curly auburn hair wild, her fair skin flushed. The older boys capture her easily, and I watch as they lead her by the elbow to the makeshift jail, a stuffy gardening shed under our deck.

I wonder what will happen next, if I should maybe intervene and release her, but she's not in there thirty seconds before she bursts out and hurtles herself at little Dylan. She's all arms and legs and nearly bowls him over with her well-muscled enthusiasm. He blushes as Katie shouts, "I surrender! I surrender!"

Dylan has no idea what to do with this armful of surrendered girl.

Later I joke to Marty, "I *surrender*? Yeesh. I have to teach Katie how to play hard to get."

As soon as I hear it aloud, I know he will laugh at me. He does. "Or we could hire someone to teach her?" I modify. "Or google it? *How to play hard to get.* Someone must know." We giggle together at the imagined danger of teenaged Katie on the loose. Katie "I do it" Abdou will not take parental instruction well.

• • •

This too is the Kurt Vonnegut brand of humor. Marty and I laugh about manageable threats instead of crying about the unmanageable ones. Not that I believe our little town has the kind of danger embodied in Graham James. Most of the adults involved in Ollie's teams are parents of Ollie's teammates, families I've known for decades. Nobody would describe them as "weird," at least not in the euphemistic sense of the word.

Only one coach causes me any true concern.

Let's call him Bub.

Coach Bub cares about hockey, perhaps a little too much. His fellow parents keep an eye on him, but mostly our concerns can be classified as minor. He allows his own kids too much ice time, taking advantage of his position of authority to give them an unfair advantage. He's overly gruff with the less talented players. He's pretty obnoxious to the moms. Already this weekend I got the Coach Bub head wave. Down on my knees, lacing Ollie's skates, I saw Bub come into the change room. I quickened my pace, knowing Bub to be no fan of moms in the change room (likely he's also not a fan of tying fifteen pairs of hockey skates but the irreconcilability of these desires — a mom-free zone *and* a team full of players with tied skates — has not occurred to Bub). I'm ready for the Bub-dismissal when he meets my eyes. I brace myself against it. He lets his eyes land on mine for a second and then tosses his head toward the door behind him, his chin drawing a sharp line from me to the exit.

You: out. GIT!

That's what the gesture says.

And do you know what I do?

I git. I scurry out the door before Bub has time to say, "Hi, Angie. Nice to see you. Thanks for tying Ollie's skates."

Ha.

In the stands, I'm livid. We all are. We're a murder of angry hockey moms, cawing at the injustice of Coach Bub. "He said —" "He told me —" "He did —"

Most of our Bub concerns fall in this category: mildly offensive, impolite, and implicitly sexist. The worst charge against Bub is that he hit a kid, a nine-year-old boy, over the head with a hockey stick. "But the kid was wearing a helmet." The dads always add this footnote. The moms never do.

Again, Canadian law states: a person commits assault when he intentionally applies force to a person, directly or indirectly . . .

Hitting a kid over the head with a stick qualifies as an application of force.

Here's what happened: as the team stood in a circle listening to Bub set out the rules for the next drill, one boy's attention wandered. Bub pulled that attention back with a sharp whack on the helmet.

The team's other coach is my old friend Trevor, a hockey player from way back. He played for the University of Regina Cougars when I was a first-year undergraduate there in 1987. Trevor tells me that in the seventies and eighties nobody thought twice about smacking a kid on the helmet.

"That's the way they did it back then."

But Trevor says this like he's telling an in-joke. Together we run a tally of other things that have changed since "back then." We share our memories of driving on the highway, no seatbelts, a dozen kids piled into a truck bed, a six-pack of beer ("road pops") between the driver's knees. We share some of the phrases on which kids of our generation were raised, warnings like, "Do I have to show you the back of my hand?" or "This is going to hurt me more than it hurts you!"

"Coaches whacked me on the helmet dozens of times. Hundreds of times. And look at me."

• • •

We can laugh. We survived the eighties, more or less intact. But nobody laughs about Bub. It's different now, and we are slowly realizing that this kind of thing was never okay. The boy's mom — Sharon — complains. Sharon deserves the gratitude of her fellow hockey moms for being the kind of mom we can count on to complain. Sharon is loud and demanding. She holds coaches and parents to a high standard. She voices her disapproval. Because I know she will do so, I don't. I don't have to. Sharon has called me on my reliance. "Why do *I* always have to be the nag?"

It's a fair question. Why don't we all work together to create fair and safe and non-stressful environments for our children and their families? Why do I do nothing but scurry when I get Bub's sexist head wave? We accept too much. Thank goodness for Sharon who does not.

In *Teaching Bullies: Zero Tolerance on the Court or in the Classroom*, Jennifer Margaret Fraser shares the experience of her own son bullied by basketball coaches. He and his teammates came forward with complaints but received little helpful response from teachers, administrators, or the ministry of education. Instead, the boys were revictimized. Into this story of abuse, Fraser embeds research on the long-term effects bullying has on the teenage brain. Ultimately, she argues that coaches should be held to the same standard as teachers. Coaches have the same power. As a society, we've become quite firm on our zero-tolerance for bullying between children. Why would we show more leniency toward their coaches who should be more mature and more responsible? We would not be okay with one child hitting another over the head with a stick. Why are we okay when the coach does it? Sharon works as a teacher and sets her standards high, for the kids and the adults. She emphasizes that adults should, of course, model appropriate behavior for the children. Bub's strike connected hard enough to make her son's eyes water. After practice, the boy's head still hurt.

This time, Sharon's "nagging" pays off. Bub gets called before the board for hitting a player. The president temporarily forbids Bub from being on the ice alone with the kids.

• • •

We enter this new season on alert for the worst, but the Labor Day weekend three-on-three tournament goes fine. We've had troubles other years. The three-on-three is not an official league tournament and not governed by the same rules. Parents sometimes take advantage of this flexibility to stack teams. They mix the best players from town with some out-of-town ringers. In their enthusiasm to win, these overzealous dads exclude nine-year-old players with soft feelings. Boys and girls who don't shine on the ice or haven't earned that best-friend status find themselves without a team or filling in the roster for a visiting out-of-town team. That happened to Ollie last year. He couldn't understand why he played on a team of Sparwood kids, none of whom he knew, while his hometown team — led by Bub, who did not extend an invitation to Ollie — boasted players from Cranbrook, Lethbridge, and Edmonton. What does a parent say to those tears? *Sorry, Ollie, but Coach Bub really likes to win, and you're not good enough.*

This year, though, we're saved from Bub. A sensible parent-coach steps in and does the kind, sane thing. He puts out an invitation to the *whole* team. First come, first serve. Easy.

The kids play hard, but the tournament is only that: play.

I stand by my promise to ensure Ollie always has an audience, and I sit in the stands for every game. But I don't do so with any enthusiasm. It's like watching practice or a casual street hockey game. There's nothing at stake. Sometimes the kids try. Sometimes they don't. I've realized it's no fun watching kids who don't try. Or even really care. Their lack of enthusiasm leads to my boredom. If it's simply play, that's fine, but they can do it without me spectating.

Also, without that competitive edge and team rivalry to excite me, I have less tolerance than usual for the mom shrieking. Marty has worked out a soundbite to explain Ollie, the highly sensitive child, to new people we meet: "His nervous system is more sensitive than most people. Sounds seem louder. Smells seem stronger. Crowds seem more crowded. He even experiences feelings more intensely than the average person. Because of this sensory and emotional overload, he is easily overwhelmed." I want to write it on a card and hand it over now in the stands, to explain *myself*! To apologize for my own behavior. My own nervous system is not ready for cowbells on Labor Day. I'm reminded of a very well-cultured, non-sporty friend who went to his nephew's hockey game and said to me afterward, in a scandalized tone, "They had *cowbells*! It was *preposterous*!" After the game, he told his nephew, "I love and support you, but I will not be at any more hockey games." *Uncivilized* was the word the friend used in conversation with me.

As the season wears on, I will ease my way into hockey and its hyperbolic lack of civility, but I'm not ready for it yet. I sit on the wrong side of the ice with a copy of Camilla Gibb's *This Is Happy* and feel mildly ironic.

I see the mothers across the rink, but I can't hear them. I hold a pen in my hand so everyone will assume that I'm busy rather than rude. My Facebook pings!

We're over here! On this side!

Then my text goes.

Look up! We're waving!

Come over!

My social life takes place mostly on the road, at writers' festivals. Here at home, I'm not exactly bombarded with invitations, so I'm grateful for these ones, even if they're only to the other side of the rink. And I like these moms. I really do. But I'm not ready to be part of them and their cowbells and their team jerseys and their home-knitted toques bearing their children's numbers — I'm not ready to be part of hockey culture — not yet, not on Labor Day weekend, not when it's a sunny thirty degrees a single wall away from this hockey ice.

My dad does nothing to improve my attitude. He mutters away all weekend about the good old days and the absurdity of this hockey weekend and the parents' over-investment in their kids' activities.

"You've organized their play. This isn't high-level competition. You don't need to be sitting in the stands, watching every move. The refs — stopping the play every two minutes — it's all wrong. Just let the kids play. When we were boys, we walked down to the pond by ourselves." My dad grew up in a rough Moose Jaw neighborhood without a father of his own. I suspect he got in more trouble than he's confided in me. My only hint into the nature of that childhood are the poorly drawn blue ink tattoos on his right arm — a three-dimensional cross on his forearm and a scribble on his bicep. They look like they were drawn by a grade-five kid . . . because they *were* drawn by a grade-five kid. My dad wasn't much older than Ollie when he and his friends decided on do-it-yourself tattoos. He always told me and my brother that the scribble read *J A* — a J for Justin and an A for Angie. I believed him for longer than I should have. Now I realize it must be *F A* for Frank Abdou, his name. He's embarrassed of the tattoos and mostly keeps them covered. But I watch the *F A* scribbles slide in and out of his sleeve as he rants. I watch the tattoo instead of meeting his eyes. "I could put on my own skates by the time I was five," he continues. "We played four hours every day — big kids, little kids, everybody. That's where we learned to love it. That's where we got good. We didn't need parents hovering over every move. Let them *play*."

In the months that my dad lives in a suite right below my own living quarters, I imagine him grumbling down there, his complaints bubbling up to me like a message from my own unconscious. I translate the message to mean *Parenting: you're doing it wrong.*

Partly, I recognize my father's criticism for what it is: delusional nostalgia. Nonetheless, I am quick to compose my defense. Times have changed. We can't leave kids unattended out at the pond all day. It's not safe.

True. Maybe.

But kids *at* the rink under Graham James were not safe either.

It's not enough to protect kids from strangers. We also need to protect them from people they know, the people in whose care we place them. We need to protect them from the "small d" dangers as well as the "Big D" ones. Recent research highlights the prevalence of bullying behavior in coaches and its long-term effects on young athletes. In a 2011 study called *The Experiences of Children Participating in Organized Sport in the UK*, the authors interviewed 6,000 young adults aged eighteen to twenty-two years about their adolescent experience in sports, and three-quarters of them reported at least one incident of emotional harm. One-third of those identified their coach as the main source of harm. Researchers in the field have begun to call out people like Trevor and me, parents ready to laugh this behavior off as "old-school." It's time to acknowledge that shaming kids, berating them, name-calling, and whacking them with sticks is not simply old-fashioned; it's harmful and no longer acceptable.

Really, though, I am talking about two different kinds of threat: macro as embodied in Graham James and micro as embodied in Bub. I am concerned with how readily we — how readily *I* — let the latter pass. I complain about hockey culture to people with no power to change it. If I don't stand up to the bullies, how can my son? I need to be more like Sharon. I should not scurry away. I should not hide behind — or let others hide behind — words like "weird" or "old-school." I am capable of standing up, facing Bub, and saying, "You do not chase the dads out of this room, and you cannot chase the moms out. Your behavior is sexist. Our children — boys and girls — need to be able to participate in this sport without being exposed to sexism."

I can't even imagine myself saying that.

But I'm going to try. I'm going to channel my inner Sharon rather than hiding behind the real Sharon. If I let people like Bub set the accepted way we act and speak to each other, what am I teaching Ollie? If I pass people like Bub off as "old-school," I'm not that different than people who passed Graham James off as "weird."

I can't be at the rink all the time, though, and Ollie is too young to call coaches out on their subtle abuses of power. I see the appeal of having a parent-coach, a dad who can hover and watch in a culture that warrants hovering and watching. Marty will never coach hockey, but I feel better when I see Trevor on the bench with Ollie. Trevor knows Ollie and has Ollie's best interests at heart. Trevor can talk Ollie down when he gets worked up. Trevor won't chase Ollie's mother out of the dressing room or whack Ollie over the head with a stick. This kind of relationship — my confidence in Trevor and, stemming from that, Ollie's growing comfort with Trevor — works as another benefit of sport, the widening circle of trust, the group of mentors that coaches, at their best, can be.

Jennifer Margaret Fraser concludes her book about the abuse her son experienced on the basketball court with guidelines for coaches, ones she makes parents responsible for enforcing. She includes rules like: a good coach should not use humiliation or embarrassment as a coaching tool. A coach should not raise his or her voice. A coach must genuinely care about the well-being of *each* athlete. A coach has winning in perspective and defines success in appropriate ways. A good coach is friendly, non-defensive, and approachable. A coach should make athletes feel good about themselves. A coach does not act out feelings or insecurities on the athletes.

I would summarize Fraser's rules thus: a coach should not be a jerk. We parents should not let coaches get away with being jerks. Hockey has a ways to go.

When the three-on-three tournament winds down, we invite Trevor and his wife, Isabel, over for a bonfire. Their two kids run wild with ours. On a night like this one, we feel lucky. We're surrounded by beauty. Our kids look happy. We know exactly where they are and who they're with.

The boys had fun at the hockey tournament, but they're having more fun now. We don't need to hover, to watch every move. We let them be kids. Their shouts and laughter stretch farther away from the fire, but marshmallows lure them back for an occasional check-in. If they go quiet for too long, one of us will go into the forest and down the hill to find them. Until then, we relax into adult talk.

Like most ex-athletes, Trevor enjoys an audience and knows how to hold attention. We all lean forward in our seats and listen to his amusing anecdotes. It's a funny paradox of my social life that the writers are quiet introverts and the jocks are the good storytellers.

Trevor stands about six feet tall with wide shoulders and a confident posture. Long lashes frame his big brown eyes. He's quick to smile. But his real appeal doesn't come courtesy of these superficial, physical traits. Rather, Trevor seems comfortable in his own skin, fully inhabiting his body in the way of athletes, or even ex-athletes. Because he's so completely at ease, he puts others at ease. I feel comfortable with Trevor, relaxed. He has that effect on women and men alike.

Tonight, Trevor talks about hockey, and we all listen. His combo of experience and confidence makes him an authority. Of course it's easy for me to grant him that authority since he says what I already believe. *Have fun! Try hard!* is his sport philosophy, his pre-game pep talk.

"None of these kids are going to the NHL," he says. "Let's be sane." I agree emphatically. I am one hundred percent for sanity.

Because of my brother's recent visit, and its revelation, our conversation comes back to Graham James. Trevor played in Saskatchewan for decades, so he has his stories too, things he saw, things he heard. Our voices falter. This conversation seeps some of the beauty and joy out of the night. Pedophilia makes a bad match for the last bonfire of summer.

"Yeah, James was weird," Trevor says, signaling the end of the conversation.

There's nothing to say for a while. The moon has risen high above the Lizard Range, and it's time to draw the evening to a close, but we don't want summer to end. We listen to a coal train come and go down in the valley. Then it's quiet.

"Where are our kids, by the way?" Isabel poses the question without any true sense of alarm. We can't see them, but they won't have gone far. They can't find much trouble to get into around here anyway. We all had our kids close to the age of forty, and we have the older-parent tendency to hover and overprotect. I'm glad we've let them wander off tonight. Kids need to explore, to learn self-reliance and resilience.

I gesture toward the sprawling forest. "Oh, they're down there somewhere." I inject a faux lightness into my voice, mocking my own nonchalance. We can laugh because we believe we have no reason to worry, but what if something has gone wrong? What if one them has fallen on the train tracks? What if they've been careless in the dark streets? What if they've run into bad people? What if any one of those dangers has befallen them and here we are drinking by the fire and laughing about the fact that we're not too sure where our kids have gone? If anything goes wrong, people will be right to put my question back on me: *where were the parents?*

The parents were doing their own adult thing and not paying very close attention. It's not easy to strike the perfect balance between being responsible but not hovering.

"Luckily, we know everybody." Trevor smiles. "The only predators around here are furry with sharp teeth."

Oh, how we all want this to be true.

We laugh with Trevor, but it's not the deep belly laugh I'm used to sharing with these friends. This time our laughter comes out tinny and short on air. It fools nobody.

As one, we turn our gaze to the sky and look for a lone star on which to pin our wish.

Please, let them all be safe.

CHAPTER THREE

"YOU CAN BE ANYTHING!"
OR LIFE AS A CORNY
MOTIVATIONAL SPORT POSTER

Ollie decided not to try out for the A team. I'm glad. I say it over and over and over again. "I'm glad. I'm glad. I'm glad."

Ollie has no problem articulating his reasons for preferring the B team and feeling no pull whatsoever to the so-called rep team.

"The A team travels more," he says. "I don't like traveling. I get car sick."

True the rep team does travel more, true Ollie doesn't like traveling, and true Ollie does get car sick.

I can think of other good, non-barf-related reasons to avoid the A team. Steering clear will mean we won't have to deal with the parents who have NHL aspirations for their kids; it means Ollie won't be exposed to Coach Bub with his tendency to whack

57

players across the helmet with his stick; it means more of our weekends will be free for skiing.

But.

Ollie could still go to the tryouts, if only to take advantage of the extra ice-time. He could hold off on the final decision until after he earned a rep-team position, if he even did. Some kids will do that. They will make the A team and then, mostly for their parents' financial reasons, will decline the spot.

But perhaps I regret Ollie's easy forfeit of A-team status for reasons beyond the three extra practices. Looking ahead to the season, the players on the A team will get more ice-time, higher-level competition, and more games than the B team players. In that way, the divide between the good kids and not-so-good kids increases every year. Self-selecting the B team will solidify Ollie's spot in the second group. I recognize my own contradictions here. My head knows the logic of letting my son decide for himself how hard he wants to push, but my own upbringing, neurotic drive, and longing for external affirmation push me to more competitive territory, even for my kids.

In many online hockey association newsletters and blogs, male coaches defend tryouts and cuts, offering parents and athletes strategies to deal with the pain of rejection. These (usually American) articles emphasize that the implicit, if not explicit, goal in sports is to win. They argue that to win — to achieve excellence — the best kids must play together.

Meagan Frank, elite athlete/coach and author of *Choosing to Grow for the Sport of It: Because All Kids Matter*, disagrees. She speaks out against imposing the stress of tryouts on young athletes. The goal of elementary-age sports should be to instill confidence in all athletes. Dividing players into tiered teams does not work toward this goal.

Ollie's decision, though, means our family will avoid the tryout drama. My relief at taking a pass on the stress of tryouts, and on the potential tears of failure, wrestles with my disappointment.

At some level, I feel that by not even trying, we're falling short. That remorse niggles at me even though I *know* I don't truly want the time and money commitment that goes along with tryout success and a rep-team spot.

I'm not the only parent with conflicting feelings about the A team. In the stands, the tension runs high. The moms claim to worry mostly about hurt feelings.

"Last year, when Michael didn't make it, he cried for three straight days. He wants this so badly."

"Jacob can barely fall asleep at night. He's so worried he'll be cut."

"Shane didn't even eat dinner. He says he wants to try out . . . but I just can stand watching him like this. The stress!"

They're just kids — that's the refrain of the mom-talk. *Our poor babies.*

The dads express misgivings too, but of a different variety.

"How much is this going to cost us? If they make the A team?"

"Well, it's more," answers a dad whose boy played A team last year.

"How much more?"

"A couple grand? At least. It's the tournaments that'll get you. You know how that goes. Hotels, meals, gas. It adds up to a grand pretty quickly."

"How many extra tournaments?"

"That depends how gung-ho the team manager is. Some try to get the team in somewhere every weekend. Lethbridge. Medicine Hat. Osoyoos."

"Osoyoos?! Osoyoos is *six hours* from here!"

"Yep. And Medicine Hat is four."

"Fuck. So much for skiing."

"Yep. Say goodbye to skiing."

The dad anxiety seems to stem partly from uncertainty. They don't even know what they'll be committing to when they let their kids compete at this level. They don't know the number

59

of weekends away, how much money, or how many lost skiing opportunities. I calculate two hockey weekends will cost at least one thousand dollars. There could easily be two tournaments a month, maybe more. How does the average middle-class family come up with an extra thousand dollars a month?

In the summer, I had contrived a plan that would have allowed us all to avoid this A team/B team debacle. The tryouts, the hurt feelings, the extra cost, the dangerous travel: all gone. My authority to be the one posing such ideas at the hockey rink amounts to approximately zero; regardless, all through July and August at my fire pit, I pitched my plan to the hockey dads. It was a sane and sensible idea. Over beer and roasted marshmallows, everyone treated it as such. My idea went like this: what about if we simply did not have tiered hockey in Fernie? What about if we divided the kids into two equal teams?

That doesn't sound too crazy at all, does it? The plan had many merits. We would have avoided the stress and disappointments that come with tryouts and cuts. We could have let kids play on a team with their good friends. We could have decreased hazardous winter travel. If Fernie had two roughly equal teams, they could have played in the same league. We would have had some games where neither team had to travel. With two teams in Fernie, a team in Sparwood/Elkford, and at least one team in Kimberley, we could have had a whole league in which nobody ever traveled more than ninety minutes for a game, and mostly travelled less.

I came up with this idea as a regular hockey mom, simply thinking about what would be best for my son and his friends and their families, simply wondering what would allow them to enjoy the sport with manageable impact. Upon looking at the research, I find that experts agree with me. In *Choosing to Grow for the Sport of It*, author Meagan Frank argues that the practice of tiered teams for kids under twelve needs to be changed, not just in hockey but in all sports. Instead of imposing the stress of tryouts and the hierarchical approach, coaches of younger kids should work toward instilling confidence in *all* players. Franks emphasizes that dividing kids into "less than" and "more than" groups does not work toward this goal and can even be "incredibly damaging to kids." The A team/B team divide builds feelings of incompetence and inferiority. Children do not understand that they might grow out of their B or C placement. Many of them take a cut as a permanent label of "YOU SUCK." I remember failing to make provincial swim teams, failing to qualify for national championships, and failing to live up to this notion of athletic success, a notion so fully realized in my own brother. I know the sinking humiliation that comes with internalizing this "YOU SUCK" label. I also know the harm that internalization does to the enjoyment of the sport, the quality of performance, and the self-esteem of the athlete.

Meagan Frank stresses that research indicates mixing talent levels of children under the age of twelve does not prove detrimental to any of the players. Voicing another of my suspicions, Frank emphasizes that recent studies show that kids play better when they play with their friends anyway, regardless of level. In his new book *Game Change*, Ken Dryden discusses the long-term effects of concussions and argues that hits to the head should disappear from hockey. Full stop. He says that putting the players in such danger is not fair, not right, and not necessary. While any one of those criteria might not be convincing alone, all three together close the deal. The *not necessary* wins the argument in Dryden's mind: hits to the head must go. The same argument can be made for early tiering in hockey. Introducing hierarchies and excluding children at this age is not fair, not right, and not necessary. Even for parents and players who do aspire to an elite level in the future, tiering pre-puberty is not advantageous. Playing all together, playing with friends, and playing for fun will not impede future opportunities.

• • •

Over the summer, not one dad raised an objection to my immodest proposal to create two equal teams rather than tiered teams. "Yes, Angie, sure. That sounds like a great idea. That makes sense. Definitely."

Relentless as I am, I even cornered the coaches, all but Bub. I got one in the stands at summer camp, one at a bonfire in my backyard, and one on Main Street downtown. I had a long talk with each, carefully presenting the benefits for the children, for the parents, for the planet.

Definitely. Yes. Equal teams. Less travel. That makes perfect sense. Nod. Nod. Nod.

But in September, in the hockey arena, the tone has changed. Tryouts are on. The teams will be tiered.

I wrack my brain to understand the intention of this tiered system. Maybe the hierarchical approach has more to do with alpha male instinct than it has to do with rational argument.

Regardless of my relentless pitch (and the lack of objections to it), the two Fernie teams will never play each other. Ollie will be in a league with teams from Golden and Creston and Invermere. Our "normal" will include driving three and a half hours to play an Atom hockey game and then turning around to drive three and a half hours back. We will ignore the fact that the travel is not good for us and not good for the planet and not at all necessary.

What about our talks? I want to scream. My sane and sensible idea? Mostly— what about sanity? The laid-back coaches appeared receptive to my plans in the summer, but they proved equally receptive to Coach Bub's plans. I knew my notions of equality, fairness, and fun would hold no sway with the Bub types so I did not even try. In the end, the Bub-way, the old approach, sways everyone. Hockey culture in Canada is slow to change.

The only justification for tiered teams? Emphasis on *excellence*: the belief that if we don't push our kids to an elite level, they will miss out on being the best. In hockey, the best means the NHL. We all say we know our kids are not going to the big leagues. We say we want them to have fun, to practice teamwork, to get exercise, to make friends. Our actions belie our words. The children could have fun, get exercise, and make friends on two equal teams. But most sport parents, even if they won't admit it, have that niggling question: "What if my kid has real talent?"

What if practicing with stronger kids and competing against better teams will draw out that excellence?

What if "dumbing down" the leagues kills an opportunity for greatness?

Nobody will say any of this aloud. Nobody looks me in the eye and tells me my idea of a hockey utopia, where our ten-year-olds focus on fun and cooperation and equality, is idiotic. In fact, none of the dads consider me much at all as they grumble their way through tryouts.

According to Ken Campbell's *Selling the Dream: How Hockey Parents and Their Kids are Paying the Price for Our National Obsession,* the chances of making the NHL are infinitesimal. Of the *elite* players born in Ontario in 1965, 1975, and 1985, roughly 0.05 percent made the NHL. Melissa, a fellow hockey mom, insists that she has no NHL aspirations for her son but only wants to give him a sport so "he can play beer league at university." I admire her realism, but if beer league is our goal, can't they play beer league inner-tube water polo? Why (expensive, time-consuming, dangerous) hockey? And if we can believe parents' assertions about their in-check expectations around the NHL, why not avoid the tiered system all together and play the game the easy way? The truth is that most children dream of one day playing on television. At least some of their parents share that pipe dream. But it will come true for less than 0.05 percent of the country's *very best* players. In a small town like Fernie, with a population of just over 5,000, we might have one or two players per year who could be classified as elite. Maybe. That does not make for good NHL odds. These chances of future hockey fame (i.e., nearly zero) should help us make level-headed decisions about how we organize the hockey that they do play now.

The Fernie tryouts do not go well. Or more specifically, the cuts do not go well. As the final results roll in, the parental grumbling gets louder. At the end of the third practice, the coaches and manager call each player into a room to find out if he or she succeeded or failed.

Cuts are hard. I remember trying out for high-school basketball and for provincial swim teams. Not at this young age, thankfully, but as a teenager. After a week of practices, the coach would post a list of names on the wall. I gathered with the other kids, hoping to catch a glimpse of my own name on the team roster. I remember the rush of relief when I found it there. Not happiness exactly. Just relief. When I didn't see my name on a first scan, I would scan again, two times, three times. I remember the liquid burn in my eyes, the ache in my chest on the occasions I didn't make the list. I recognize those feelings now as a kind of grief, a mourning for a lost season, a lost experience, and a lost peer group. Nobody likes to be left out. Nobody likes to fail. But with the list-on-the-wall approach, those who did not see their own names could sneak off and collect themselves. I would have had time to compose my brave face. *Maybe next time*, I could tell my parents and friends. Later, after I'd recovered from the emotional impact of rejection, a good coach might pull me aside for some encouraging words and some advice on how to improve.

But not here. Fernie Atom hockey allows no such grace period. Here, each player — Derek, Jacob, Cameron, Ellie — sits alone to face the minor hockey president and two coaches. Silently, each Atom player listens to a list of his or her shortcomings.

One doesn't make it because he doesn't skate well enough.

Another doesn't make it because he's too small.

One is told that he made the A team as the weakest player so he will have to work extra hard to prove himself.

Another is told that he made the A team as the strongest player so he will have to work extra hard to prove himself.

The jury of adults base these assertions on three one-hour practices. Remember, children do not take this cut as a one-time decision influenced by coach preference and subjectivity. Nor do children understand that how they played on those specific three days might not be representative of the kind of player they always are and certainly is not representative of the kind of player they could be in the future. The kids hear this cut as a pronouncement on their self-worth. With a cut, they become of the "lesser than" group. The cut marks them: *you suck.*

The kids cry. Some cry because they didn't make it. Others cry because they did make it but none of their friends did. One cries because he's too short. The parents respond as parents would.

"Who would *say* that to a kid?"

"*Who* would say that to a kid?"

"Who would say that to a *kid*?"

News of the private backroom conversations do, of course, filter out to the other children, aggravating Ollie's sense of justice. "Why would they tell Charlie he's too small? He can't help being small! What's he supposed to do? Go *grow*?! And anyway, Shane is smaller than Charlie and Shane's not even old enough to play Atom in the first place. Why does Shane get to make the team and take a spot away from Charlie who's the right age?"

Because Shane's good for his age. Because Shane is Coach Bub's son.

If I want to put a positive spin on this experience, I could tell myself hockey provides an early lesson on life's lack of fairness and on how people with power do not always use that power wisely or kindly.

But I think we can do better than that for our kids.

The dads huddle in the stands, ball caps pulled low over their eyes, hands pushed deep in their pockets. They complain less loudly than the mothers do but with more gravitas. The serious tone and somber expressions might be appropriate in a discussion of NHL scouting reports. When I remind myself that they're actually talking about a few winter months in the lives of a group of nine- and ten-year-olds, I nearly laugh.

The dads whose sons made the team don't celebrate. A darkness pervades the conversations. There's a sense that things have not gone well. The sinister backroom pronouncements, the crying kids, the rising sense of alarm at the big unanswered question: *how much precisely is this A-team season going to cost us?*

I don't have *schadenfreude*, not exactly, but I want someone, anyone, to say, *You were right, Angie.* I want someone to say, *Your way would have been better.*

I flit about their conversations like a parrot. "Don't you remember our conversation?" I can't help myself. The dads do nod at me, exactly like they would nod at a young child. That's how much weight my words carry at the arena — my ideas equivalent to a toddler's fairy tales. *Yes, yes, sweetie, great idea. We remember.*

I wonder if the three Atom girls on the Fernie team see this sexism, if they suspect their inclusion in the sport of hockey has a similar superficiality.

All summer long when I talked, I had thought people listened. The reality of hockey culture's sexism sinks in. I might be forty-seven years old with three university degrees and a long history in sport, but at the rink I'm still "just a girl." Maybe facing that reality will be the first step to changing it.

Am I up for that fight?

Where's Sharon?

Answer: she's staying quiet through the tryouts, largely disengaged and unemotional, because she'd rather see her son cut at this stage than vulnerable to the likes of Bub for a whole season.

• • •

I will try to rally myself for this battle against hockey culture with the knowledge that much of the most persuasive new sport research comes from women, particularly Jennifer Margaret Fraser on bullying and Meagan Frank on tiered teams. These women aim to do at a national level what Sharon, my hockey-mom conscience, tries to do at the local level. I predict that if hockey culture is to change in any significant way, the impetus will come primarily from women.

I expect Ollie to fixate on this tryout fiasco, especially the detail of his nine-year-old friend being told he's too small. That's the kind of mean-spirited injustice Ollie can really grab onto tight. That evening as I head out to a library event, I say, "Ollie, about the tryouts, you have to remember that adults —"

I pause, trying to figure out what I want to say. Adults what? Adults are mostly faking it? Adults don't deserve the power we give them? Adults can be thoughtless jerks?

Before I have time to figure out a helpful conclusion to my sentence, Ollie shrugs, his mood uncharacteristically light, "Well, good thing at least that *I* decided not to go to tryouts."

Yes. Smart Ollie. He's free of the whole emotional mess. Maybe I should let him make more of the decisions. There's something to be said for the intuitive power of a sensitive boy's nine-year-old gut.

"They probably would've cut me too anyway," he says, a heaviness creeping into his voice. Already, he's internalized their "*you suck*" message.

"You don't know that." I kiss the top of his head. "You're on my A team. All-star and captain."

• • •

At the library, I attend a book launch for a novel on which I did some early editing work. I go to support the writer's debut effort, but I feel out-of-sorts. The negativity of the arena clings to me, and I arrive at the library in a mean mood. Though I'm happy to see this woman achieve her publishing dream — and though I feel good about having been able to help get her there — it's not my kind of book.

I prefer books with more complex characters and less predictable resolutions than hers has. I like new, surprising stories. Handsome rescues Pretty has been done. After the sexism at the rink, I have a lower tolerance for the rerun of this particular story than I did a year ago.

At the launch, the author talks a lot about Oprah. "I wanted to become a writer," she says, "because of Oprah. When I saw the way she treated writers just like real celebrities, I thought *I could do that! I could be a writer!*"

She chose to be a writer for the celebrity? My grumpy mood threatens to boil into a rage. I stare ahead, counting backwards from one hundred, forcing an expression that could be interpreted as a smile. I will not roll my eyes.

Writing for celebrity is like playing Novice hockey for the NHL. But worse. Even the highest caliber writers in Canada, ones who have worked hard at their craft for decades with little reward in terms of attention or financial remuneration, could not be classified as celebrities.

This woman's book has been published by a very small press. The print run is five hundred copies. The book tour consists of two hometown launches, both audiences made up entirely of friends and family. The author's chance of becoming a celebrity? Even with the fact that she's included an Oprah epigraph? Zero.

The talk of writing and celebrity provokes the same skin crawl as talk of hockey and the NHL. It's not just the delusions of grandeur that bother me. It's also focusing on an unlikely conclusion rather the rewards of process.

Suddenly I'm critical of everything. I wonder how much the author's outfit cost: all cream and lace. Fitted bodice. Skirt flaring to mid-thigh. High heels. Hair in an updo. She's dressed like a bride at a Manhattan wedding, ready for her *Glamour* photo-shoot, not like a small-publishing-house writer at a rural library event. I see now she's outfitted for her own appearance on *Oprah*. She's dressed like a celebrity.

This event is not about the writing. It's about external affirmation of self-worth.

I too have been known to overdress for library events, but hockey has put me in a bad mood tonight, and I'm especially critical of this prioritizing of status over process. Often the characteristics we most despise in others reveal the tendencies we fight within ourselves.

"I wrote a novel the way I do all things," she's saying now. "I googled *How to write a novel.* I did the same for music. *How to start a band.* Even tonight: *how to do a book launch.*"

All I have to do is survive this one evening. I bite the inside of my lip and watch the clock's secondhand tick through the Q & A. *I can do it.*

Then the yoga instructor at the back of the audience asks, "What did you learn about *yourself* in the long process of writing this book?"

I swear I hear our author answer, "People always tell you that you can do anything, and you *can't!*"

I laugh, quite loudly, but I am the only one in the room who does. I think, *What a perfect, hilarious answer.* You *can't* be anything. She can't get a big city agent. She can't get a Toronto publisher. She can't write a book that will get attention and reviews. *She can't.* But what does she do with that "failure"? She does not accept the *you suck* label. She spends eight years revising her book until a small publisher will print five hundred copies, and she finds meaning in that publishing process. She buys a pretty dress. She celebrates with friends and family. She can't be anything, but she makes do with what she *can* be.

Most kids can't make the NHL, but they can play a sport they love, enjoy time with friends, improve their fitness, and take pleasure in the challenge and in the *work* itself. They *can't* be anything, but they can find happiness and meaning in what they *can* be.

"People tell you that you can do anything, but you *can't*." It's such a refreshing and honest statement that I can't contain myself.

Life is not a corny motivational sport poster. All of that business about "shoot for the moon and even if you miss you'll land amongst the stars"? It's not true. You might reach for the moon and land on your ass. How great to hear someone say it aloud. How hilarious that she does so at the publication of her own book.

Why, then, do *only* I laugh?

Because that is *not*, in fact, what our author has said. She has answered, full of a sincerity that would please Oprah, "When you're a kid, people tell you that you can be anything and that you can do anything, and you *can*! You *can* do anything. Look at me: I wrote a book!"

For her, life *is*, in fact, a corny motivational sport poster.

YOU CAN'T BEAT THE PERSON
WHO NEVER GIVES UP.
Yes, you can.
I WILL PERSIST UNTIL I SUCCEED.
But you might not succeed anyway.
WINNERS NEVER QUIT AND
QUITTERS NEVER WIN.
Oh, shut up.

Fame and fortune are exactly the wrong reasons to write. I tell my students: only be a writer if you really can't help it, if you *love* writing. I'm talking about the same kind of Aristotelian love that I hope draws Ollie to hockey. If you're drawn to writing like an apple is drawn to the ground — if writing's gravitational pull on you is irresistible — then write.

This particular student-author did not hear me. She heard Oprah. If I could find a nearby punchbowl, I would drown myself. *You can! You can be anything!*

• • •

This sort of delusion fuels tiered hockey. Ironically, the emphasis on elitism in youth hockey works against its very goal. In a 2012 *Hockey News* article, Ken Campbell argues that elitism is, in fact, making Canadian hockey less likely to produce elite players. Many kids marked as B or C at such a young age simply leave the sport, long before they have had a chance to develop and even know their potential. This exodus leaves fewer players from which to build strong hockey programs with depth and range. Campbell writes, "It's almost as though the game has become too important to Canadians, which has in turn made it an all-in or all-out proposition. In other words, why bother continuing to play hockey if you're going to be weeded out of top competition by the time you're ten years old? When the stakes become that high, so does the commitment, and that as much as anything is what drives talented players away from the game and into other pursuits."

In the end, avoiding the tiered approach would be better not only for young kids' happiness and enjoyment of the game, but also for the quantity and caliber of hockey players still competing as they reach adulthood.

I see many parallels between the writing life and the hockey life. Both writing and hockey can be central to the formation of self. I *am* a writer. Ollie *is* a hockey player. Our very identity and sense of self-worth get yoked to these activities in a way that can be unhealthy. Managing this potential destructiveness of sport (or writing) comes down to the difference between enjoying one's life through an activity versus proving one's self-worth through an activity.

I often succumb to this misplaced competitiveness, the impulse to validate oneself through meeting external measures of success. I'm afraid that's why I resisted Ollie's decision to skip tryouts.

It's not easy to admit that I project my own complex desires, my own failed dreams, and my own neurosis onto my child.

I have something to learn from Ollie. Maybe hockey is not about identity for him, after all. Maybe he simply *likes* playing hockey, and he can happily do that (without the travel or the barf) on the B team.

• • •

While I worked on *The Bone Cage*, I had a mentor relationship with Ottawa novelist Elisabeth Harvor. I sent her a scene in which one character has a mental-health collapse because he fails to make the Olympic wrestling team. She wrote me back, "Don't you think this guy overreacts? Aren't you overblowing the drama? It's just a sport."

I replied, "But everything these athletes are is tied to that sport. The character has put his life on hold — his family, his career — and has invested years of money and energy in a quest for excellence. Now he's come to the end of his athletic career and he hasn't made the Olympics. He has to ask himself, *What were those years for? Who am I without wrestling?*" Elisabeth still didn't seem convinced, so I added, "Imagine if you turned thirty and someone said, 'You're too old to be a writer now. You can't write any more. Pick something else to do. Pick something else to *be*.'"

"Well, they can still coach wrestling."

"Yes, and you can still teach writing."

"Oh," she said, "that *is* bad."

Her response has two dimensions. Partly, it has to do with celebrity, or at least with external validation. If we keep writing until our deathbeds, we can keep the dream alive. We can believe that one day we will get the readers and the awards and

72

the adulation and the heaps of cash that we deserve. But more than that, giving up writing at thirty would be "bad" because we enjoy the process of writing (more than we enjoy the process of teaching). The work of writing lends meaning to our existence.

Here's what we can work on as parents, regardless of the activity: steering children away from the former (craving external validation, worrying about status) and toward the latter (enjoying the process, taking pleasure in the work itself). That's what I'm going to try to do — for myself and for Ollie. But I cannot control the other parents, the coaches, the president, or the league. I can only be responsible for my own son. In this case, I had only to follow his lead.

These deluded notions of success that *I* have had to fight hold no sway over my son. To him, the A team/B team hierarchy means very little. He loves to play hockey and he hates to travel. He will, therefore, play on the team that has less travel. For him, it's as simple as that. I am happy to learn one of my lessons has rooted in him: *Ollie plays hockey only for Ollie.* As a mother, I will aim to help him trust his gut and to hold on to that simplicity as long as he can.

CHAPTER FOUR

KIDS IN THE COLOSSEUM

"What are we doing here?"

"Yes. What *are* we doing here?"

"This is crazy."

"Yep, totally crazy."

Families file into the Golden, B.C., arena, parents gripping extra-large coffees and looking almost embarrassed. We laugh at the ridiculousness of our situation instead of facing it straight on, but we know we've chosen a truly silly way to spend our Sunday. We've all driven 350 kilometers for the first league game. We'll watch nine- and ten-year-olds play hockey for ninety minutes and then turn around and drive 350 kilometers home. There must be a saner way to organize our children's play, but making change — and standing up to those currently calling the shots — would require energy that none of us has. It's easier to follow instructions, to do as we're told, to drive and drive and drive. So here we are in Golden.

But I do feel excitement as the kids skate out on the rink for the first competition of the season. They look big and strong and fast. *What happened to our babies?* Moms and dads alike get misty-eyed at the difference a season makes.

Ollie still holds his stick funny, though — sort of upside down and sideways, the blade facing the ceiling instead of the rink. He likes to give his stick a little midair twirl before the blade hits the ice surface.

"That's my way of doing it," he says when I attempt to correct him.

Ollie has his own way of doing most things. I let this one go. If he keeps playing, a coach will eventually have to convince him of the ineffectiveness of his stylistic flare. In the two seconds it takes to execute his "Ollie twirl," the play has often sped by him. My competitive dad finds this exasperating, which might explain his minimal presence at the rink.

I settle into the bleachers between two hockey dads whom I trust to behave in a sane, subdued fashion. I've picked Roland as my go-to hockey dad this season. An elite athlete himself, he remains rational and level-headed about his son's sport. Roland competed as a mountain biker in the 2000 Olympic Games held in Australia, and he will be inducted into the British Columbia Sport Hall of Fame this summer. I learned about none of his accomplishments from him. Like most truly successful athletes, Roland never talks about his victories. In this post-competition, hockey-parent version of Roland, I can tell he's an athlete mainly because he's always eating.

"Do you know where we can get some food?"

"I'm hungry. Anyone else hungry?"

"Are you going to eat that?"

When I ask him about his athletic history, he talks not about the mountain of gold medals he earned, but about the toll elite sport took on his personal life.

"You have to be a little off in the head to compete at that level. It's unbalanced. The only thing I thought about for all those years was training. And eating and sleeping, so that I could train. I couldn't have a real relationship or job. I couldn't put energy into education. I could bike. That's it. You have to be a bit crazy."

I suspect my brother would agree. Though he and Roland competed in the same Olympics, they don't know each other. I find it interesting that they share a very similar, hands-off approach to parenting their own child athletes. Justin and Roland support the kids' passions and interest. They encourage physical activity. They drive the kids to practices and games, and they watch from the stands, but they apply no pressure.

Grady, Roland's son, does not go to summer hockey camp because the family reserves those precious sunny months for hiking and beaching. Roland never gets stressed if Grady misses a play, nor too excited if Grady makes one. I've never heard Roland raise his voice at the rink. He watches, calmly, a small smile playing at the corners of his mouth and shining in his eyes. He seems to find the kids amusing, whether they win or lose, skate or fall.

I wonder about Justin and Roland. Do they not push their kids because they've lived athletic success and don't need to live it again through their kids? Or do they stand back because having succeeded themselves they know intuitively what the research says: *parents do not create athletes*. If the kids decide they want that kind of sporting success, the drive must come from inside. Or do Justin and Roland not push because they do not even want that kind of athletic success for their kids? Because they know elite sport will mean an unbalanced life. They know it's crazy.

Next to Ollie, Grady is my favorite player to watch. He's a sweet kid with freckles splashed across his nose and cheeks. He's always smiling. He plays defense, and when he stands at the blue line, keeping an eye on his own team's offensive play, I can hear his enthusiastic "Go Ollie! Go Ollie!" That — the friendship, the camaraderie, the investment in another person's success, the desire to see others excel — reminds me of the good in hockey, in all team sports.

Today's game, though, does not pull my attention toward these heartwarming moments. Today, my heart gradually inches its way into my throat. I don't remember hockey being so rough. We've reached a new stage: a year older, a year bigger, a year faster, a year more aggressive. I flinch every time a little body flies into the boards with a blood-chilling thump. When a child goes down and stays down — as happens three times in the first period — I wonder again what we're doing here. Isn't it a bit barbaric for parents to cheer from the stands while these little warriors engage in full-out battle? It brings to mind the subversion and containment of the Colosseum. Within those confines, supposedly civilized humans used other humans as entertainment, forcing them to engage in inhumane and violent behavior; audiences applauded this violence that they would not condone on the streets. Similarly, we wouldn't tolerate this behavior in the classroom or at home, but at the arena we celebrate it: "Go team! Get 'em!" We might not want to think too hard about what kind of bloodthirsty impulses this display satiates.

Someone's going to get hurt! That's what I want to say. *Stop them!*

But I bite my lip. It's a stupid thing to say. Of course, someone is going to get hurt. It's hockey. Don Voaklander, director of University of Alberta's Injury Prevention Centre, claims Alberta emergency departments see nearly 8,000 hockey-related injuries per year. For kids under nine, concussion is the most common injury. More than ever before, we *know* the long-term and very negative effects of concussions.

We're here anyway.

• • •

"They don't do full-contact hitting yet, in the second year of Atom," the coach tells me, "but they learn to use their bodies more."

I cringe at the crash of two players connecting hard with the boards. I imagine there being a rather fine line between "hitting" and "using their bodies."

"Yeesh," I say to Roland. "I'm not sure my mama-heart can take a whole season of this. In fact, I don't know how I'm going to make it through the next hour."

"It's a bit rougher for sure," he says with that Roland calm I envy, displaying the steady nerves required for his own athletic success. "Injury is the part of this sport that worries me. It's not worth it. Especially when we start talking about their brains."

Roland knows all about brain injuries. He concussed himself twice mountain biking. The second one ended his athletic career. Years later, running an ATV in his backcountry driveway, he rolled off the bank. His wife, Amanda, found him with his scalp split wide open. Since Amanda works as a nurse and has experience with head injuries, she didn't take it personally when he started swinging at her. She knew her good luck when his violence turned to vomiting and removed her from danger. A STARS helicopter ambulance flew Roland to Calgary for emergency treatment. He has taken years to recover, struggling with insomnia, irritability, personality change, memory loss, and confusion. Who would want that for their child? Who would let their children play in a sport in which it's likely to happen? We will all need to think hard on these questions when our children turn thirteen and enter Bantam, the first age group with hitting and, therefore, a real threat of concussions.

"Absolutely not worth the risk," I agree with Roland. "Yet, here we are. I'm hoping Ollie picks a different sport soon. Swimming maybe. I suspect hockey will wear off. With his late birthday, he's at such a disadvantage —" Roland pokes me in the ribs as I talk and points to the ice. I watch the play as I finish my sentence, "and, to be honest, he's just not that great, which will probably get bor—" Ollie skates with the puck straight up the center of the ice, around two players, shoots upper left corner, and scores, "—ing."

"What was that you were saying about your son?" Roland's bemused smile breaks into a laugh.

"Wow." I'm full of proud-mama emotions, and I don't even try to downplay my reaction for Roland. Ollie's eyes still find me in the stands, but I know the days of him blowing kisses from the ice have gone. I settle for his quick glance my way, and I give him a subtle thumbs-up. But there's nothing subtle in the reaction I show Roland. "Did you see that? Wow!! And just when I was dissing him. Bad mom."

"They're young," Roland says. "It's too early to know who's going to be good."

Ollie ends his full-season goal drought with not one but *two* goals in the first game of his second-year Atom. His coaches recognize the jump by awarding him the golden Player of the Game jersey. Ollie seems shy about the award. Whereas most kids refuse to take the jersey off for the time it belongs to them, Ollie refuses to wear it at all. Not on the ice. Not at home. His peers show more enthusiasm for his award than he does. I interpret Ollie's lack of enthusiasm as a lack of confidence and am ineffably grateful to each of those little hockey players who generously celebrates his success.

Ollie shrugs at their cheers and compliments, but I see the hint of pride in his eyes. Those goals, this recognition, and these friends — all so good for him.

• • •

I have a secret that I don't tell Sharon (the hockey-mom I can count on to call hockey coaches and administrators on their misbehavior) or Roland (the sane former Olympian who does not pressure his own young athletes, at all) or any of the other parents. This morning, on the long drive to Golden, I bribed Ollie for the first time. Or maybe bribed is the wrong word, but I implemented a reward system.

There.

That sounds better.

Five dollars per goal. This game cost me ten bucks. I don't even have to look at the research to know this practice is flawed. Parents and coaches should reward input (a hard practice, a good effort to make a team play), not output (scoring goals).

The only reward for scoring a goal should be how good it feels to score a goal.

My dad, who suddenly views himself as something of a sport psychologist, tells me so at great length. He gives Ollie a meaningful post-game stare and asks, "How did scoring the goals feel, Ollie? Did it feel good?"

These questions irk me because I don't recall this tempered approach to sport existing in my childhood. My dad didn't ask me if I felt proud of myself for working so hard, for swimming two hours a day, for rarely missing practice. Instead, I remember him being angry when I had an off meet, and younger, typically slower swimmers beat me. I remember overhearing conversations about why he spent so much money on my sport when I didn't stand out as a star, when I wasn't as good as my brother. I remember him not coming to my competitions because my performance did not impress him. I remember feeling invisible except when I screwed up.

Would you like to know how that felt, Dad?

Even Ollie seems skeptical of this "how did it make you feel" version of my father.

"Yeah, it felt good, Grandpa," Ollie says with no enthusiasm and bolts. As he rounds the corner, I think I hear a muttered *duh!*

Ollie's goals do make for a fun start to the season, but my niggling discomfort at the rougher play sticks with me.

Really, I'm lucky. Until recently, Canadian kids this age engaged in full contact. The history of body checking in hockey is filled with controversy, and the age for legal hitting has shifted in both directions as a result of debate and research. In 2002, Hockey Canada decided to let nine-year-old players body check. The decision ignited much debate and a year later, in 2003, the league moved body checking up to Pee Wee (ages eleven and twelve). More recently, both USA and Canada have been experimenting with moving body checking to higher age groups. Quebec doesn't permit it until Bantam (ages fourteen to fifteen). Interestingly, Dr. L. Syd Johnson, a specialist in neuroethics and traumatic brain injury, emphasizes that — despite this difference or maybe *because* of it — Quebec is the only province in Canada that has seen growth rather than decline in the number of children playing minor hockey. In 2013, Hockey Canada again raised the minimum age of body checking from eleven to thirteen nationwide.

According to an academic article by University of Toronto's Anthony Marchie and Michael D. Cusimano, legal body checking accounts for eighty-six percent of all injuries among players nine to fifteen years old; players in contact leagues are four times as likely to be injured; and most injuries are caused by legal checks. Hockey causes more concussions than both wrestling and football. In fact, when it comes to the number of concussions, hockey stands above all other contact sports as the clear leader. The concern comes into sharper focus when we acknowledge that doctors and medical researchers now know that the developing brain is at greater risk of injury. Dr. L. Syd Johnson states the case most directly: "The fact is that the vast majority of concussions, and hockey injuries overall, at all levels of play, are caused by legal body checking. It's safe to say that as long as body checking is part of ice hockey, a high rate of concussions will also be part of hockey." Reports show that despite the improvements in equipment, the number of youth concussions in hockey is increasing.

Nothing has made me want to grab Ollie and run from hockey more than reading the research about concussions.

I understand the arguments of the other side. Most of the time, I *am* the other side. Until now, I had been excited for Ollie to reach a league that allows body checking. He enjoys the more physical play, and I enjoy watching him enjoy himself. I've said all of the things parents say when they attempt to justify full-contact sport.

We can't bubble wrap our children.

Kids need to learn to move through the world as it exists, dangers and all.

Body checking is an important part of the game.

If they start young, they can learn to do it right and protect themselves.

Boys will be boys.

Boys love roughhousing. It's FUN.

You know what's not fun, though? Nausea, anxiety and depression, learning disabilities, personality changes, suicide, and early dementia. Concussions cause all of these things. These symptoms morphed from abstract to real for many hockey fans in 2011, when three NHL enforcers died tragically within four months and doctors publicly linked the causes to on-ice brain trauma. NHL tough guy Georges Laraque, who I got to know during CBC's Canada Reads, remembers looking at his peers' photos in the newspaper and wondering, "Am I next?"

• • •

My brother also experienced concussions while wrestling at the international level. He tells a story about being in the locker room after practice in 1992, while his teammates talked about an upcoming competition. He sensed the tournament's importance from their tone but couldn't quite grab hold of the conversation. He couldn't remember where they might be competing and whether or not he'd packed a suitcase. With panic mounting, he asked in his best imitation of casual, "Hey, guys, what tournament?"

They laughed. "The Olympic trials." A couple young men looked uneasy, but most of them figured Justin must be joking around.

"Am I going?"

Was he going? He was favored to win. He'd been thinking largely of nothing else for the last four years. The laughter grew more uncertain.

Because Justin really couldn't locate this information in his brain, he got aggravated and confused. His teammates' laughter made him angry.

Later, he realized he'd gotten "a little concussion" at practice. He'd "just rung his bell."

Even knowing what we know now, some parents and coaches still talk about head injuries this way.

While parents, coaches, and league officials do debate the whens and hows of body checking — should hitting start at nine or eleven or thirteen? How soon should players return to the ice post-concussion? How serious does a concussion have to be before a player is pulled? — recent medical researchers do *not* engage in these particular debates. Rather, medical researchers largely speak with a unified voice. The cost of concussions in youth is high; hockey has more concussions than any other sport; legal body checking causes the vast majority of those concussions. The solution? The *only* sensible solution? Ban body checking. University of Toronto's Marchie and Cusimano, for example, argue that parents are asking the wrong questions. We should not be asking when to return to play but whether to return to play — and not how to include body checking in minor hockey, but if.

Large medical organizations support this shift of thought.

The Canadian Academy of Sport and Exercise Medicine has officially stated that checking is not necessary for play at minor hockey level. The American Academy of Pediatrics recommends limited body checking among players younger than sixteen years. Some doctors even recommend banning hitting until kids have finished growing and are able to sign their own consent forms, at the age of seventeen or eighteen.

• • •

While I'm preoccupied with thoughts of bruised brains, my high-school friend Alanna visits me from Moose Jaw. With her boys on the verge of leaving home — one to university and the other to a hockey prep school in Notre Dame — she wants to spend a week "breathing the same air as them." She sells them on the idea of this week with Mom by promising mountain-sport adventure in my little town. The family of four meets me downtown for a coffee. Approaching fifty, Alanna and her husband, Mark, have gotten hooked on CrossFit. Both wear clothes that display their enviable fitness. Alanna mostly danced in her youth, but she also did well in high-school sports like volleyball, basketball, and track and field. Last time she drove through my town, we met at the playground so her boys would be distracted by monkey bars and slides while we talked. On this trip, two men — one of them over six feet tall — look at me with Alanna's eyes.

Alanna's husband, Mark, played junior hockey himself, but he is unlike Justin and Roland, who have stepped back from their children's games and are content to watch from a dispassionate distance. Neither Justin nor Roland pushed their boys to adopt the father's sport — wrestling and mountain biking, respectively — instead encouraging the children to find their own sports. Mark, on the other hand, introduced hockey to his boys at a young age. His reasonable explanation for doing so? "I wanted to give them a lifelong sport. People don't play senior men's football. Or geriatric wrestling. Hockey's fun. Guys play it for a long time. I remember my last game in Junior. We lost. My teammates — twenty-year-old men — were crying in the change room. I thought, *I'm done with this sport.* I kicked my bag away to the corner of the garage and didn't touch it for six years. Then I picked it up — I've had great times in hockey since then, made great friends."

"When he moved to Moose Jaw, where I'd been *my whole life*, he instantly had more friends than me," Alanna agrees. "All through hockey."

• • •

Looking at Alanna with her two children on the brink of adulthood is a glimpse into my own future. If I'm lucky. Polite and respectful, her boys sit quietly while we converse about their origins in hockey. Trying to include them, I turn to the younger one, the hockey player: "Notre Dame! Wow. You must be good at hockey. You love it?"

It's an obsession of mine. This relationship between love and sport.

The talk of hockey lights him from the inside. He steps out of his shyness and meets my eyes in a way that hints at a confidence not immediately apparent off the ice. He nods. *Yes, he loves it.*

"That's the way it's going," Mark says. "Prep schools. Last year, Saskatchewan had nine Bantam prep teams. This year it has thirteen. It's a new attitude. More like Russia. That kind of focus, letting talented kids excel, giving them access to resources."

"A cheque-book sport." I'm parroting the research I've been reading. "Hockey's becoming a rich-kid sport. Parents who aren't affluent can forget about hockey for their kids. Twenty thousand dollars a year, I read, for these schools."

"Yeah. That's true. That's the bad part. Twenty thousand before boarding costs."

It costs Mark a bit to admit this, the bad part. He and Alanna are flying pretty high on their son's success, buoyant with pride as any parents would be. But Alanna and Mark both work as school teachers, and with the funding of two university educations on the horizon, they don't have endless resources for a hockey school like Notre Dame. They've promised their youngest son one year at Notre Dame, after which he will go back to Moose Jaw to play AAA Midget, with the boost provided by a hockey-focused prep school.

"We've always made sure hockey was their choice," Mark says. "They take me to practice. That's how we did it. I don't take them to practice. They take me. Our oldest had had enough by grade seven. He quit. Fine."

I like this idea. *You take me to practice, Ollie.* If it's important to the player, he can remember the schedule. He can watch the clock. He can pack his stuff. He can tell me when it's time to go.

In short, the player makes the commitment, not the parent.

Mark and Alanna work with kids for a living. Their boys seem smart and mature and kind. In the face of all this sanity, I wonder what Mark and Alanna think of hockey injuries, of concussions, of body checking.

"Oh, you could talk about that issue all day long," Mark says. "On both sides. Hitting will always be controversial."

I push because I'm curious what sort of story a good, loving father tells himself as he sends his youngest son off to a high-pressure prep school in a sport that consistently records the highest number of brain injuries. I ask the question knowing full well that I might do the same if Ollie ever shows the potential and the desire. "When I read the frequency and effects of concussion, though . . ." I say. "Sometimes I just want to take Ollie and run as far away from the rink as I can get."

Mark shrugs then, but the gesture seems neither aggressive nor dismissive. He's not shrugging the matter off nor making light of my concern, not exactly. His son had a concussion last season, he tells me, and sat out one game.

"I didn't want to, though," the son intervenes, breaking his polite silence. "I could have played."

Mark shrugs again. I can't decode the gesture. "Hockey leagues are extra careful now," Mark agrees with his son. "Not every concussion is a big deal. But they treat every one that way. He had a bit of a headache at most. The league takes every precaution."

He just rang his bell.

Mark's son came into Pee Wee (ages eleven and twelve) just as Hockey Canada moved hitting up to Bantam (ages thirteen and fourteen). The second-year Pee Wees had a year of experience body checking and then had contact taken away.

"But do you think the change is good?" I ask. "To be safer, knowing what we know?"

The answer surprises me. "No," the boy says, "I would've rather learned to hit earlier."

"If they started in Pee Wee," Mark says, "they would learn to do it right. Learn to keep their head up, learn to protect themselves, learn body awareness. And in Pee Wee, the size difference between kids isn't so great. By Bantam, some kids have grown and others haven't. They have no experience hitting. But they're fast and slamming into each other. Kids get hurt."

"Some doctors make a similar argument about size," I venture, "about the big differences in height and weight between kids at some age groups. But the doctors argue hitting should *wait* until all kids have finished growing — until seventeen or eighteen. Then players will be old enough to sign consent forms and to legally agree to subject themselves to danger and potential lifelong harm."

The boys exchange a quick glance. They stay quiet and polite, but they disagree with me. I can see that.

"You think that's stupid, right?" I ask gently. "Holding off on hitting until seventeen?"

"Yes." They answer immediately and in unison. I wonder if hockey culture speaks through them. They're still impressionable young men, and hitting is part of that hypermasculine world. I remember feeling invincible at their age, and I wonder if they can truly understand the lifelong consequences of traumatic brain injury.

Mark shrugs again. I interpret the gesture as an acknowledgment of the issue's complexity. The casual up-and-down movement of Mark's shoulders doesn't mean "I don't know" or "I don't care," but something more like "I *can't* know."

"Then again," Mark finally says, "Quebec has always waited. They hit late. And Quebec always sends a bunch of kids to the NHL. You could argue it all day. Both sides."

• • •

When I get home and ask nine-year-old Ollie his opinion on the debate, he of course agrees with Alanna's boys. "I think we should start hitting early. To learn how."

"In Pee Wee?"

"No, in Atom."

Right. So good thing Ollie is not in charge. He'd have them all hitting at eight years old. Like other kids born late in the year, he was eight for most of his first year Atom. As absurd as this idea sounds — as much as full contact for eight-year-olds is the brainstorm of a roughhousing boy with no understanding of long-term consequences — hockey leagues *have* allowed kids as young as eight to hit.

Hockey is a different game with the hitting than without the hitting. I've seen that even with Ollie's young age group. Some star kids back right down and become invisible as soon as play turns rough. Sometimes they go straight to the bench, not interested in engaging at all in the body contact. Other kids, the ones less agile but stronger, suddenly shine. Since body checking is part of the sport at elite and professional levels, kids who aspire to that level want to learn how to do it right. They want to play the real game. They don't want to work hard until fifteen or sixteen or seventeen and then find out they're the kind of player who disappears when on-ice play gets physical. I get it. Through the eyes of Mark and his boys, I can understand why some argue for the inclusion of hitting as young as Pee Wee.

But when I hear a young player's body crack hard into the boards? When I see a kid motionless on the ice? I have to agree with the doctors.

In a comprehensive 2003 study on body checking and concussions in youth hockey, Anthony Marchie and Michael D. Cusimano put the responsibility for change on physicians, concluding "eliminating body checking could refocus the game on fun and skill — on skating, shooting, passing, and team play. Physicians must play their roles as socially responsible citizens: the future of our youth and the game depends on it."

Of course, hockey is not the only sport with inherent dangers. Any sport done to a high level results in injury. Bodies are not meant for that kind of intensity or that kind of repetition. Elite sport does not translate into great health and wellness. Elite sport translates into excess, and excess comes with a cost. Even non-contact swimming ends with bad backs, bad knees, bad necks, and bad shoulders. Both Marty and I, still in our forties, have arthritic shoulders. Marty had both acromioclavicular joints removed at the ripe age of twenty-one. I went through a year when I couldn't empty the dishwasher without my shoulder clicking out of joint. But let's not pretend injured shoulders affect life quality in the same way injured brains do. In the words of Ken Dryden, speaking about *Game Change* at the 2017 Vancouver Writers Festival, "A leg that limps is one thing. A brain that limps is another."

In 2002, pathologist Dr. Bennet Omalu discovered chronic traumatic encephalopathy (CTE), a degenerative brain disease caused by hits to the head. Omalu says no kid under eighteen should play contact sport. His latest study examined brains of 111 deceased football players and all but one showed signs of CTE, a condition marked by memory loss, depression, and suicide. Omalu elaborates on the dangers of head trauma in his book *Truth Doesn't Have a Side*. If a child plays a game with contact to the head, the child is more likely to die before age forty-two. The long list of NHL tough guys to die before fifty since 2010 includes Bob Probert, Derek Boogaard, Rick Rypien, Wade Belak, Steve Montador, and Todd Ewen. In November 2017, the *New York Times* published a heartbreaking series of messages to sports reporter John Branch from the father of Stephen Peat, a thirty-six-year-old defenseman heading down the same path of depression, violence, drug addiction, illegal behavior, irrationality, and suicidality. The threat of danger became so extreme that the father, Walter Peat, broke off contact with his own suffering son. Walter Peat attributes his son's behavior to head trauma sustained in hockey: "Stephen is deteriorating fast, living on the street, has pretty much zero help from NHL, and my relationship with him had gone south [. . .] I am a normal person who loves hockey, but to see what the game has become, and the end result of the vio-lence allowed on the ice — the worst is the fact that most sports teams are still in the dark as far as recognizing the health risks associated with many sports. The rule book must be rewritten." The father's desperation and despair increase with each message as his son's situation becomes increasingly dire and their alien-ation more complete. His final message concludes, "As I respond to this, Stephen is texting me right now, begging for money. Says he can hardly lift his arms, as he is so weak, starving, cold, but still blames me for all that has happened to him. Some days, I find this whole nightmare like a bad dream, wishing I could wake up, and it was all over."

I think of Dr. Omalu's study as I read this story about the Peat family. Dr. Omalu asks, "If you love your son and daughter, why would you intentionally expose him or her to the risk of permanent brain damage?" Omalu instructs parents to put this question to themselves: do I love hockey more than I love my child? Parents of Walter Peat's generation made their decisions without the hard facts on concussion. We have those facts. Now we need to close the gap between awareness and action.

"Why, knowing what we know, is nothing changing?" I pose the question to a local doctor whose son suffered a debilitating concussion, precipitating the whole family's big step back from excessiveness in youth sport.

"Because they're obsessed! The parents!" Even now, a year after her boy's recovery, she's emotional when she speaks. "It's about the parents' sense of self-worth. They take status from their kids' excellence in sports. It's gone beyond all reason. I saw a girl hit in the head with a soccer ball and I told them, 'Get her off the field. She's got a concussion. Look! She's holding her head.' Nobody would do anything. I had to remove myself from the situation. Parents: they're completely, irrationally obsessed. It's not about the kids."

For the health of our children, doctors and medical researchers must continue to raise awareness of the serious dangers of head injuries and the prevalence of those injuries in hockey. They must continue to fight against body checking. So too must parents, if we love our children more than we love hockey.

Hockey Canada's current rules give me two years. In that time, I will educate Ollie. Together, he and I will hopefully make the right decision: hitting or no hitting? Hockey or no hockey?

In the meantime, I hope the research and advocacy of Dr. Johnson, Dr. Omalu, and Ken Dryden bring about real change in the culture of hockey, change that leads to the implementation of rules to radically reduce the threat of head trauma, for the sake of our children.

CHAPTER FIVE

HOCKEY-MOM GUILT

I skip around the house belting out lyrics about leaving on a jet plane and not knowing when I'll be back again.

"That's not true, Mom. You do know when you'll be back. You'll be back on Thursday."

I'm going to Austria. And I'm downright gleeful about it. Generally, I've shaped a yearly cycle that follows my snowbird parents' travel cycle. I do most of my book travel in the summer and fall when they're here to help with childcare, and then when they go to Mexico, I stay home. I can do that, I tell myself: I can stay put for the length of a winter. I can focus on kid schedules and meals and dishes and laundry from November to April. That's doable.

But I *can't* do it when I get an invitation like this one. I'm off on an all-expenses-paid trip to Innsbruck, Austria, where I've been invited to an alpine arts festival to speak about my ski-town novel *The Canterbury Trail*. And I am downright giddy.

Stepping out of the mom cycle and into the role of writer gives me room to breathe. Ollie and Katie have a curious way of talking about "Angie Abdou, the writer," as if she's someone different than "Mom." Angie Abdou, the writer, travels a lot on planes. She does things like write novels that appear in book-stores alongside other novels, even some by famous people. "Mom" just nags about vegetables and bedtimes and oral hygiene. Like every other mom. I'm grateful for the opportunity to be "Angie Abdou" every once in a while, and I'm ecstatic for this early December trip, which is a blatant cheat on my promise of a winter at home as "Mom."

I throw my suitcase in the trunk alongside Ollie's hockey bag and we drive to the rink. He's got an early morning game, and it's opening day at the ski hill, so Marty and Katie aren't coming. They plan to squeeze in a few runs before relieving me at the arena sometime around the third period so I can run to the airport. The other moms resent the bounce in my step. Today I will do it all. I will sell the 50/50s. I will shriek with the other parents. I will man the penalty box. I will swing the damn cowbells. *Preposterous* or not, I will do it all with rampant enthusiasm because the exit sign is in clear sight.

"I'm leaving after the second period," I say, "because I'm going to Austria." I say it like I would say I'm going to the grocery store. *Austria*, no big deal, just going there, at third period.

I've never been to Austria before, and I don't even know what to imagine. I haven't invested any time in figuring out. I know only that I won't see a dishwasher or a laundry room for nearly a week. Various Austrian people will be tasked with entertaining me, filling *my* needs, and ensuring I have a good time. Such pampering seems impossible from where I'm standing now, square in the middle of motherhood.

For Marty, I've left my usual three-page single-spaced list of instructions. It details where the kids need to be and when and who to pay. Marty will be saddled with a fair amount of hockey duty while I'm off "gallivanting through Europe," as he puts it.

Marty, who leaves the house every morning at six to supervise the environmental department at a coal mine, has a hard time taking parts of my work seriously. Understandably, keeping fish alive seems more important, more *real*, to him than traveling the world to talk about made-up characters. "Maybe I'd quit forgetting to call these trips 'work,'" he said, "if your 'work' wasn't always called a 'festival.' Maybe you should call it a 'workival.'"

I refuse to engage. Hours until departure.

I do sometimes wonder whether me staying put more often would mean Marty and I would have to work out these sticky points in our relationship.

Marty grimaces into my hummed rendition of "Leaving on a Jet Plane," not finding me especially entertaining.

"Relax," I say (because that's always good, helpful spousal advice in marital disagreements). "It's my last trip of the winter. I'll be home January, February, and March." Already it feels like a sentence.

"You'll be home until something else comes up. Something else always comes up."

"I'll say no. I'll have to. We have no childcare over winter."

"You didn't say no to this."

"Well, c'mon, it's *Austria!*"

"Right."

"I'll bring you chocolate."

"Great. Thanks, Ang."

The moms in the stands mirror Marty's hostility. "We hate you," Roland's wife, Amanda, says. She's the most cheerful person I have ever met, her face lifting upwards in a permanent smile. She works as a nurse, and I imagine her as the best. Amanda's good nature and the cheerful twang of her Newfoundland accent soften her words. "You get to go places. You get to do things. With no kids! All of us moms *hate* you. Take us!"

I barely absorb the game. It's pretty even. Ollie's improved since last season. He doesn't fall or drop his stick, key features of last year's performance. He's right there in the play, as he has been most of this season. Or I should say, he's right *alongside* the play rather than *in* it. He's near the puck but doesn't seem to have the hutzpah to take it. *Pretend it's your puck*, I've advised him before other games, as if some notion of politeness holds him back. He seems to follow the play rather than anticipate the play. I say this, let me be clear, fully aware that I know absolutely nothing about hockey. Every parent: an expert.

I spend most of the two periods working the penalty box with a dad of a first-year girl on the team. There's a defeated slouch to his shoulders. He looks penned in by more than the hockey boards. Originally from France, he moved to Fernie for the athletic outdoor opportunities, but life has had its way with him too. He didn't move to Fernie to spend Saturday morning inside, sitting on his ass and ensuring the time clock dwindles to zero. Yet here he is. As we perform our duties, he tells me about Innsbruck. "They love Christmas. Go to the market. The mountains are marvelous, but they won't be skiing there yet. Not this early." Neither of us mentions Fernie's opening day at our local resort, where I know he'd rather be.

As soon as Marty and Katie appear at the glass, in matching toques and bright faced from some fast runs at the hill, I leap to my feet.

The moms boo at my back. "The rest of us are *slaves*," Amanda yells. If I said that, I'd sound bitter and angry. Amanda's delivery somehow makes *slaves* sound like a punchline in the funniest family sitcom. Without a single glance over my shoulder, I wave, cocky, arm above my head. I am gone.

• • •

On the one hundred–kilometer drive to the Cranbrook airport, I dwell on this morning's conversations until the glitter begins to wear off my giddiness.

"You're going away again?" Ollie has a way of saturating his words with indignation, bafflement, and despair. He might as well ask, *You're feeding me rat poison again?* He ignored his breakfast and glared at my packed suitcase as if its appearance this morning was the first he'd heard of my trip.

"For a little while. Barely a week, Ollie."

"You're missing my game?" He hadn't touched his peanut butter sandwich or his banana, his lack of interest in food hinting that this drama was not all for show.

"I'll be there for most of your game."

"And back for my tournament?"

"I'll be back in time for your next tournament."

"WHAT?" With true despair in his voice, he asked: "What is the point of even having a mother when she's never even home?"

Ouch, Ollie.

I laughed a little at his melodrama. I imagined Marty using the same line: *What is the point of even having a wife when she's never even home?* I knew then that I would quote Ollie often, to comic effect. But I also knew he had a point.

I could never say I'm a slave to marriage and motherhood with her lightness. I could never make my incarceration to domesticity sound like a bit of good fun, the way she does.

Once I get some distance from the rink, I see the injustice of leaving Marty with this game and tournament. Despite my earlier judgments of Marty and all my talk of being *the* hockey parent, the sport truly has become a full family commitment. I might have been the parent to make the decision to allow Ollie to play, but Marty bears his share of the responsibility, without ever having signed on for it in the first place.

• • •

We all struggle with this balance between responsibility and desire, between commitment and freedom. Last week, out of the blue, my dad said to me, "We divided kid responsibilities. Mom did the swimming with you, and I did your brother's sports." My dad's expression was new to me. Vulnerability? Maybe. "Your mother was the swimmer. I was the wrestler. It made sense. A lot of families did it that way. Dividing kids. We had to do something. That's what we did."

"I know, Dad. I get it."

My dad had never apologized to me before. Never even tried to explain himself. But that's what I heard in these words. For me, the conversation-behind-the-conversation went something like:

Him: Sorry I paid no attention to you.

Me: I understand.

Him: We tried our best.

Me: I know. I get it, and I forgive you.

Whether or not he wanted my forgiveness, he got it. Years of resentment floated up and out of my body.

Several years ago, my dad told me a story about leaving his young family to compete in an international wrestling tournament. My brother and I were still toddlers. On the way home, my dad stopped in the airport gift shop to grab us presents. A rifle for my brother, a doll for me. "I was just a kid," my dad said. "I didn't know anything. I thought, boy: gun; girl: baby. I didn't have the slightest clue how to be a father." He was in his fifties when he told me that story, but in his face I could still see the lost twenty-one-year-old boy trying to figure out what it meant to be a parent.

I feel the same.

• • •

A psychologist friend from Massachusetts once told me that the hardest part of being an adult is realizing that you only get to live one life. He's right. I want them *all*. All of the lives. In my early twenties, life was nothing but choice, a five-star all-you-can-eat smorgasbord. But I made those choices — career, husband, kids, hometown — and one by one, I chose myself into a box. I have managed to maintain two competing lives: "writer," which involves wearing pretty dresses to glamorous festivals with open bars, stimulating adult company, and attentive audiences, and "mother," which involves staying home and ensuring a secure and reliable and predictable routine for my wonderful family. But too often I feel torn in a way that prohibits me from fully enjoying either life. Each time I step into one role, I experience an uncomfortable, anxious guilt at abandoning the other.

When my kids were younger, I had one of those debilitating crises of confidence at the Saskatchewan Festival of Words. "I should be home with Ollie and Katie," I told my friend Dave Bidini over a post-event glass of wine. "They miss me when I'm gone. I haven't put my suitcase away in a month. They're still so little. They need me."

"I've never understood that attitude," Dave reassured me in a gentle, placating tone. "The idea that you should change because you have kids. Why not be the best you that you can be? Why not let your kids get to know that you? Show them how to chase their dreams by you chasing yours."

I clung to Dave's advice in the following years. In airport lounges, on runways, in hospitality suites, on festival stages, packing and unpacking and packing again: *the best me I can be.*

I have repeated Dave's words so often, they've become a mantra I live by. *Let my kids get to know the best me.*

And my kids have, as they've grown, gotten to know writer me. They're proud of me in their own weird way. "Angie Abdou, the writer" might be someone different than "Mom," but she's someone they feel lucky to know and claim as their own. Ollie, who is obsessed with memorizing the chronology of various significant events, can recite the publication dates of each of my novels. To Ollie and Katie, a career in the arts is a real thing, a possible and admirable vocation. They're always working on novels of their own (Katie's first, penned when she was five, had the particularly powerful and intriguing title of *Bliss Falls into a Death Pit*). Though I envy their speed of composition and detest their blithe "There! Another book done! My third today!" I do love that they see writing as a worthwhile and respectable use of time.

Point Dave Bidini.

Years after the Saskatchewan Festival of Words, I had an opportunity to thank Dave. "That meant so much to me, what you said about not giving into mom guilt, not succumbing to subtle societal pressures. I decided to follow your advice and let my kids get to know the best me I can be."

"Oh, that," Dave shrugged, seemingly modest in the face of my effusive gratitude. "You should never take me seriously when I'm high."

I still don't know if Dave was joking, but I don't regret following his advice. I'm proud of my (modest) accomplishments, and I'm glad I've maintained a life beyond my role as mother, for the example it sets for both my daughter and my son, but it's never easy. Even now, when Ollie and Katie are seven and nine and need me less, it's never easy.

• • •

I miss them as soon as I settle into my plane seat. It's not a pleasant kind of missing, not a glowing appreciation and gratitude, not a gentle longing. It's panic.

"I just came from my son's hockey game," I tell my uninterested seatmates. "I left before it even finished. I stayed until third period, though, and almost missed my plane. I'm skipping a tournament while I'm gone too."

I know I'm being ridiculous, delivering this unsolicited confession. I can't wait to go. I can't wait to get back. I'm the anti-Buddhist: always absent in the moment.

Recent scientific research indicates that after a mother gives birth, the baby's DNA becomes part of her body. That child's DNA remains with the mother into her old age. I imagine that little bit of my babies tucked snugly beneath my breastbone. I feel it there. The farther I get from the living breathing children, the greater this bit of them inside of me stretches. The longer my trip, the more intense the ache, the more wrong my departure feels. My children tether me to home in a way that hurts.

On this trip, hockey tethers me to home too. In Austria everyone asks me about hockey. When I tell them I came straight from my son's hockey game and will return straight into another hockey road trip, I confirm their sense of what it means to be Canadian. Innsbruck, home of the 1976 Winter Olympics, is a sporty town, and my hosts and I talk a lot about children and athletics.

The people I meet, academics, have a moderate view of youth sport.

"My granddaughter was quite good at gymnastics, but once she got to a certain level it took up too much of her time. She wanted to try a variety of sports."

"My brother prefers the arts to sports. He's more of a reader and writer. But we try to keep him active. We focus on general health instead of competition."

"My friends and I used to ski race, but now we ski tour — it's more about getting out and enjoying nature and exercise. Less pressure."

"Skiing is a popular sport here," people tell me over and over again, as they gesture at the magnificent rocky peaks, only a sugaring of snow at the very top. But I don't meet a single person involved in ski racing.

These Austrians — glowing as they describe the joy they experience in their pursuit of outdoor recreation — remind me of home. Innsbruck is beautiful the same way Fernie is beautiful. I play the dutiful guest and ooh and ahh at their mountains. They want me to be impressed, and I understand that wanting. I do the same to my guests in Fernie.

So I look at the Innsbruck mountains, and I say, "Wow, so beautiful," and I mean it. The Austrian Alps truly are beautiful, of course, but I want to pull out my iPhone and show them pictures from my own kitchen window, from my bedroom. My Canadian Rocky Mountains elicit the same kind of awe, the same grounding awareness of the insignificance of humans, the same reverence for the natural world. I'm embarrassed I needed to come this far to be reminded of the beauty of my own mountains.

In the same way, I needed this distance to gain some perspective on my family life. So I use my time away from kids and their sports to think about my kids and their sports. I think especially about different countries' attitudes toward athletics and where Canada fits on the spectrum. China is perhaps the best example of an extremely competitive approach to young athletes. There, the government assesses children's physical attributes at a very early age in order to direct them toward the sport (and the intense sport schools) where they will most likely have success. China makes United States seem relaxed and nurturing in its approach to youth sports, but I know from my brother's experience that American youth programs are still more intense and competitive than their Canadian counterparts.

In his early teen years, my brother attended U.S. wrestling camps where he trained all day long. The focus was on producing national champions who would hopefully go on to become world champions. Kids who didn't keep pace were called "losers" or "pussies" and were humiliated in front of their peers. Adults took a pack animal approach to sport. Some coaches and parents punched or kicked kids for failing. Wrestling was a tough sport, the story went, and these adults believed themselves to be in the business of making tough kids. *Go hard or go home. No pain, no gain.*

But Americans themselves have begun to question their overly competitive attitude toward youth sport. John O'Sullivan, author of *Changing the Game: The Parent's Guide to Raising Happy,*

High-Performing Athletes, and Giving Youth Sports Back to Our Kids, argues, "The general rule is that [children] should never be involved in more hours of organized sports [per week] than their age." He also explains that parents should expose children to as many different options as possible, "but wait as long as possible for them to find the sport that's best for them physically and emotionally, and then support them as they chase their dreams." O'Sullivan argues that the adult obsession with winning has become the enemy of excellence in sports. The goal should be to prioritize the player experience over the needs of adults.

Many countries have begun to question the focus on elite sport at a young age and suggest it has the opposite effect to what we might hope. For one, this notion of excellence may lead to inactivity in the vast majority of children who don't display obvious talent in their youth. Secondly, contrary to its very aims, focusing on excellence too early reduces a country's star athlete output by reducing the pool of athletes. In 2015, Judith Woods from the U.K. wrote an article called "Not on the team? Then no more sports for you." Woods argues that competitive sports have declined in schools to the extent that sport has become an elite-only activity. She calls the disappearance of recreational sports a national scandal: "Despite Coalition promises of a lasting Olympic legacy that would see a generation 'inspired' to get active, a new survey by the Youth Sport Trust has depressingly revealed that pupils nationwide spend significantly less time in sport and PE classes than they did four years ago."

Innsbruck, I learn, faces similar issues. The country's citizens bought the concept of hosting the Olympic Games on the promise of improved health and wellness for the country's youth, but now the focus is on how the government can use the infrastructure to bring in tourist dollars rather than increase physical opportunities for the general population. Innsbruck does host many youth competitions at these great facilities, but those events focus on a very small group of elite athletes. They do not encourage kids to "get out on the hill" to get some exercise and have fun. Health and wellness experts argue that athletic associations should not even stage national competitions for prepubescent children. Woods emphasizes that in the United Kingdom, despite promises of long-term and widespread benefits from hosting the Games, rates of physical activity have not risen and twenty-six percent of boys and twenty-nine percent of girls are overweight or obese. Parents lament the fact that if kids don't make the team, their participation in physical activity is eliminated entirely. Woods calls this approach "nurturing the best and ignoring the rest" and resents the clear message it sends to kids that sport is only for the elite. Kids who repeatedly fall short of making the team know themselves failures by the time they turn eleven years old. This statistic hurts: in a little over a year, my own boy faces this sporting doomsday.

• • •

So what can we do? What would positive change look like? Again, we need to close the gap between our awareness and our actions. We know that to thrive kids need downtime and unstructured play. In 2006, Olympic rower Silken Laumann published *Child's Play*. In it, she offers a guide to reconnecting with our children by letting kids be kids. Laumann fondly recalls playing hide-and-seek or kick-the-can until her parents called her in after dark, and she laments that today's overscheduled children don't enjoy this same freedom. She blames busy lives and intense societal pressure to turn our kids into superstar athletes, academics, and artists.

Yes, children need more free time to play, to wander, to explore, to imagine.

But also, within organized sport, we need to shift the focus more to fun, friends, and fitness. We can make room for playfulness even in the competitive realm. Refusing the pull toward elite athletics at a young age will help.

In a 2017 article, John O'Sullivan (who is also the founder and CEO of the Changing the Game Project) suggests a radical 180-degree shift in the way we view sport. He asserts that our biggest mistake is focusing on talent selection rather than talent identification. Most coaches, he argues, *select* talent when they should be *identifying* talent, and the difference does great harm to the USA's future talent pool. The culprit, he says, is too much emphasis on winning at a young age. "Talent selection is the culling of players with the current ability to be successful in events taking place in the near future. Talent identification, on the other hand, is the prediction of future performance based upon an evaluation of current physical, technical, tactical qualities. Talent selection is pretty simple; talent identification is an art." Talent selection leads to great results now. Talent identification helps build "elite athletes and winning teams for the future." To support his argument, O'Sullivan points to Piotr Unierzyski's study on junior tennis players. Unierzyski evaluated twelve- to thirteen-year-olds competing from 1994 to 2000 in fifty different countries. His pool included future stars like Roger Federer. Unierzyski's analysis revealed that the athletes who eventually made it into the top one hundred professional rankings were often younger than the mean age for the group, slimmer and less powerful than their age group, played fewer matches than the top age-group players did, practiced less than the elite players, and had supportive but not overly involved parents. In other words, there is no obvious way to identify the "Roger Federers" of the world when they are twelve or thirteen years old. Moreover, those "Roger Federers" do not become stars because of overly frequent competition or because of the pressure of pushy and ambitious parents.

Given the shortsightedness of singling out young athletes and pushing them toward greatness before they have matured physically, why do so many of today's coaches favor talent selection? Because they're not looking to the future. They want to win now. O'Sullivan stresses that the win-at-all-costs youth sport culture means that seventy percent of those young athletes have quit sport by age thirteen. O'Sullivan stresses that the seventy-percent dropout rate "is why the emphasis on winning prior to high school is destroying youth sports . . . [and] . . . why nations with 1/100th of [the USA's] population can compete with [Americans] on a world stage in many sports." Sweden, which does not cut any hockey players until age seventeen, produces more NHL players per capita than any other country. Other nations have begun to learn from Sweden. Youth sport should focus on fun, participation, and skill acquisition, *not on excellence*. We know this, right? So what gets in the way? Ugly human impulses. Adult thirst for victory. Voyeuristic enjoyment of childhood success. Desire to proclaim our kids better than other kids. Dreams of fame and riches.

I do not hold myself above such impulses. I'm critical of Ollie in ways I shouldn't be. I'm sometimes frustrated by his way of holding his stick with the blade facing the ceiling, his habit of shadowing the play but never having the confidence to lead a play, his reluctance to take the puck, and his nervous tendency to pass right in front of the net when he could take a shot himself. I should be praising his enthusiasm, his effort, his love of the game. That's all I should be doing. I've come this far to see myself clearly. I had to travel all the way to Austria — 8,080 kilometers — to think honestly about my treatment of my own kids. Occupying the "Angie Abdou" space, I am able to have a good hard look at "Mom."

I am no perfect hockey parent.

• • •

My Austrian hosts don't work me too hard. The one classroom visit on my schedule gets canceled because of a professor with a head cold. I'm left with a one-hour lecture to give on the last evening of my stay. Mostly, I eat. I do breakfast with one group, lunch with another, and dinner with a third. Sauerkraut. Wiener schnitzel. Goulash. Beef soup. Dumplings. Because my grandma spoke German, I always refer to her as being of German descent. In this food, though, I remember that her parents came from Austria, not Germany. The flavors make me nostalgic for family. I want to run home and make the kids apple strudel. Instead I go with my host for sachertorte and admit to myself that this particular trip really is more festival than "workival."

At home, Marty breaks his "no rink rats" rule and takes Katie along to the tournament in Whitefish, Montana. He has no choice. My Montanan writer friend Susan, whom my family has never met, is away for a few days and offers them her vacant home so they can save on hotel costs. The text messages roll in: pictures of Ollie and Katie squished together on Susan's expensive massage chair, pictures of Ollie and Katie smiling over heaping bowls of ice cream at Whitefish's make-your-own-sundae place (gummies, marshmallows, Smarties, *and* chocolate sauce), pictures of Ollie and Katie snug in sleeping bags on Susan's sectional couch.

Marty and I get along better by text. "XOXO," he writes. "MISS YOU," I respond. If only real life were this easy. Nothing but block caps love.

My TeamSnap app beeps throughout the tournament too. I'm so far away, yet the second Ollie scores a goal, I know. The second he gets a penalty, I know too.

I should be there. When Ollie scores a goal, I want to be the one his eyes find in the stands. When he gets a penalty, I want to be right there to see that he's okay. I want to ensure he's not having a complete meltdown because the referee's call was "unfair." Why am I in Austria, drinking schnapps and eating chocolate, when I should be in a Montana hockey arena preposterously ringing a cowbell?

I get other messages from home too, like the one from my friend Randall Maggs, author of a brilliant book of poetry about the legendary goalie Terry Sawchuk. In response to our ongoing conversation about hockey and my questions about how I decide how much energy to invest in kid sport, Randall writes about his own son's participation in ski racing:

> *What I remember is whenever David's big Atlantic ski race, the Marble Cup, and the music festival were on the same horrendous week in March. One day he had his two slalom runs and two music classes. We had to race back and forth between Marble and the Arts and Culture Centre, a fifteen-minute trip. Jean-Claude Killy and Debussy. Get harder on your outside edge and be lighter on the black keys. He'd do the first run, then come on the stage to play the piano in his skins. Running back to the hill after that first run one of those crazy days, trying to pull his ski boots on in the jeep, his hands slipped and he put the boot through the windshield. We knew then something had to give. Either sport or music. But his decision. Some time around then, I saw that Tim Raines came down off his bedroom wall and Beethoven went up. There's more, but I'll keep that for a phone call or over a small round table some day with a couple of pints of Guinness.*

That's poetry isn't it? Harder on the edges, lighter on the keys. The boot through the windshield. Tim Raines replaced by Beethoven. But I wonder if the parental philosophy ("his decision") is clearer in retrospect than it is right inside the craziness. I wonder if Randall felt less clarity while he spent those days shuttling, days away from his writing, his skiing, and his wife.

My one-hour talk for the Austrian audience goes well. I put on a good show and earn my keep. The audience cooperates. They nod appreciatively at my observations and laugh loud at my jokes. They make me feel like a stand-up comedian, and I grow taller and more confident into their laughter. They buy all my books. Someone in the audience is from Alberta, and she and I connect over our mutual admiration of NHL enforcer Georges Laraque. She tells me we also share an interest in the limits of the body and

107

the meaning of sport and that I've inspired her: she will follow her dream of writing. Not all literary events are life-affirming and confidence-building, but this Austrian event is one of the best.

It's been pretty fun being "Angie Abdou, the writer" for a little while. I'm glad I got to see the Innsbruck mountains. I'm glad the Austrians liked me.

But I miss *my* mountains. I miss my Ollie and Katie.

Goodbye for now, Angie Abdou.

I'm going home to be Mom.

CHAPTER SIX

UNTIL HOCKEY
DOTH US PART

I land in Cranbrook to heavy snowfall. Other passengers stagger into the warm light of the waiting area and then into the arms of smiling friends and family. Nobody greets me. I lug my bag into the dark and dig my car out from under the meter of new snow. I curse the icy wind and the snow falling so hard now I can't even see across the parking lot. I dread the drive home to Fernie.

I have a history of bad luck on these mountain roads. In a spring blizzard of April 1999, a Rossland boy, overly keen to get to Calgary to see his girlfriend, pulled into my lane to pass a snowplow and crashed head on into me at full speed. I broke my back (the L4 vertebra) and spent four days in the trauma ward of the Calgary Foothills Hospital, not knowing if I would ever walk again. After x-rays and tests, doctors released me with a clamshell body cast. I did walk again, within the week, but I lived with chronic pain for years. The accident took place ten days before the Boston Marathon, for which I had qualified, registered, and trained. Five years passed before I ran a race of any distance again. I'm lucky to be able to run at all.

But I don't regret that accident. I wouldn't even undo it. Until then, I lived a life parallel to the one I most desired. I wanted to be a writer, a novelist. Instead, I worked as a PhD student at the University of Western Ontario, analyzing and teaching other people's writing. I liked that life for its proximity to what I wanted. Teaching and writing about great fiction came close enough. I had never even tried writing fiction myself.

That evening on B.C.'s notorious Highway 22, when I saw headlights coming straight toward me through the snow, I thought, 'That's it, I'm dead. Game over.' Those two words actually passed through my mind as if I valued my own life no more than a pinball game.

When I woke in the trauma ward, friends and family expected me to be depressed. No Boston marathon for me. Instead of running in the world's most famous distance race, I lay stoned on morphine, facing years of rehabilitation and chronic pain. Depression seemed an appropriate response.

But I felt pure euphoria. *I'd lived!* I had said goodbye to the world at my first glimpse of those headlights, and here I was. Still here. As soon as I left the hospital, I bought a stack of how-to-write manuals and began trying my hand at fiction. Life could end at any time, with no warning. I saw that now. I would not waste my time. I would not avoid my real goals because I feared failure. Imagine never even trying to do what you most want because you're too chicken?

Five years later, in 2006, I published my first book. In 2018, I published my seventh.

So, despite the long-term physical pain, I would not undo that accident. It gave me the life I wanted. But that does not mean that I would want it to happen again. It hurt. The recovery process took far longer than I would've liked. And I've had other accidents since then without the epiphany and without the transformative outcome. In 2005, on this very highway from Cranbrook to Fernie, I hit an elk, first with my car and then with my face. It smashed over my front bumper and through my window, rolled across my hand on the steering wheel (for twenty-seven stitches to my pointer finger), came crashing over my face (for twelve more stitches above my lip and a broken nose), and finally buckled the roof of my Subaru before falling to the side of the road. The RCMP said if the elk had been smaller than its estimated 800 pounds, it would have come straight through the windshield and killed me. It didn't quite fit, lucky for me and anyone who loves me.

I hit that animal after dark on the way home from proctoring a December exam at the College of the Rockies, around ten p.m., like tonight. With the elk's dark torso facing my way, I didn't even see it. The clunk of its body against my car was my first indication that something had gone terribly wrong. After that accident, driving at night felt like Russian roulette. At any moment and without notice, death can jump out of a ditch and hit you in the face.

So I do not like to drive. I'm not very good at it. It scares me. All the way home from Austria, I fantasized about Marty offering to pick me up. *It's dark, sweetie, and snowing hard. Driving will be dangerous. You'll be tired. I'll come get you.*

Admittedly, that would have been silly. I have a car at the airport.

Plus it's poker night, and Marty is playing cards and drinking in some friend's garage. I get a text: WELCOME HOME! DRIVE SAFE. Out Late. See you tomorrow! XOXO

After a stressful drive, putting all my trust in the red taillights in front of me because that's the only thing I can see, I finally make it home to dishes on the counter and laundry on the couch. Travel

111

and jet lag have made me irritable. I know what Marty would say, *You can't go away and leave everything to me and then criticize.*

Apparently, I can. I throw some dishes around, huff up the stairs with an overloaded laundry basket, and crawl my lonely self into my lonely bed.

In the morning, I'm up at six to take Ollie to Creston for a hockey tournament. He has three games today. It's still snowing and my mood has not improved.

Ollie hates mornings, so I bring him pancakes in bed and wake him up gently. Still he whines.

"Ollie, I flew in from overseas last night. I got up before you. I made you breakfast. You *cannot* complain."

"But why not? I *am* complaining." He infuses his words with absolute misery. On days when Marty and I are on the same team, Marty's there laughing by my side. *The sooner we can get this kid on coffee, the better,* Marty would say. But today I am alone.

"Why would they give us a game so early?" Ollie grumbles into his pillow as I try to pull him from sleep, pancakes soaked in maple syrup on his nightstand. "Don't they know we have lives?!"

• • •

"Laundry's all over the place," I greet Marty when he makes his hungover way downstairs. I won't look him in the eyes.

"Yeah, it was a tough week, Angie. A little busy here at home. At least I did the laundry." His tone is tense too. Neither of us gets the homecoming we imagined. But we're both too cemented in our own resentment to be the one to take a first step toward what we really want, a hug. So much of this morning could be fixed with a simple *I love you.* Those three words would melt the resentment.

The air is so thick with tension, walking through it hurts, but I push my way to the door. "We're going," I say to the wall. "If they make the finals, we won't be home until Sunday night."

112

Neither of us has done anything especially objectionable, but we're electric with instinctual antagonism, fur on the back of our necks rising. I claw and hiss at him. He growls and foams at the mouth in response. We're both ugly with anger.

"Okay, have fun . . ." Marty's words lift up in a question mark. I imagine his question to be something like: *what the fuck is your problem?*

"You'll have to take Ollie to practice on Monday night," I snap. "I have a library board meeting."

"Sure. No problem. What time?"

"Hockey is at five thirty on Monday, Marty." I can make a simple sentence so mean. I don't even know the source of all this anger.

"Do you have to be so condescending?"

"Hockey is always at five thirty on Monday. It's been at five thirty on every Monday since September."

"You know what, Ang? I'm not you. I can't hold it all in my head. I can't do it all. I can't be at work and manage hockey and feed the kids and put the fucking laundry exactly where you want it while you're off traipsing through Europe. I'm asking what time hockey is because I want to know. If you want me to quit caring, to quit trying, keep answering like that."

Admittedly, he makes some solid points. This would be a good time for me to apologize. *Sorry. I'm just tired from travel. I hate driving at night. The storm scared me. Thanks for doing everything while I was gone. I appreciate you.*

Traipsing through Europe? "We're going. C'mon, Ollie. Bye, Katie. I love you."

"Bye, Angie." Marty too can make simple words turn mean. His tone says, *Really? We're going to do this now? What is wrong with you?*

"Fuck you, Marty."

"No. Fuck you!"

Oh, the sweetness of marriage. I get in the car and turn off my

113

phone. There will be no block caps reconciliation today. I'm tired of an electronic life so at odds with our real one.

"Mom." Ollie's voice comes quiet, tentatively, from the backseat. "Why do you and dad sometimes seem like you hate each other?"

"I'm sorry, Ollie." I will not cry. I have 250 kilometers of winter driving and a weekend at the rink. If I start crying now, I don't know how I will stop. "We don't hate each other. We're just tired."

"Well, why don't you take a rest?" That's Ollie — always thinking of a solution, always trying to help. Other people's pain hurts him more than it should. I know Ollie more than anyone, and I should behave better than I do. But, god, I'm exhausted. I feel the fatigue as an ache in my bones. I'm so tired my face hurts.

Would a rest even help me and Marty at this point? We're so sick of each other.

Or, no, that's not true. Not exactly. We've forgotten each other. At "Mom" and "Dad," we're doing pretty well, most of the time. "Angie" and "Marty" both have some great moments, succeeding in careers, sometimes beyond what they'd imagined for themselves. But "Husband" and "Wife" — those two have slid into oblivion. "Lovers" — not so much. We're busy. The refrain of contemporary family life: *so very busy.* "You're right, Ollie. We should all take a rest. When hockey's over, we'll go on a big holiday. Maybe we'll go see Grandma and Grandpa in Mexico."

But first: another weekend apart. Marty's Grandmother Jean told me never to go to bed angry, and I'm going to Creston for a whole weekend very angry and very hurt.

• • •

Hockey works to divide couples in this way, almost always. The children on Ollie's team all have one parent in the stands, the other busy elsewhere with the remaining demands of family life.

Much ink has been devoted to instructing spouses how to

co-parent a hockey player after a divorce, how to divide the financial obligations and time commitments, as well as how to create a situation in which the athlete can thrive rather than being affected by negotiations around the marital collapse. However, there is no research that suggests the blame for these divorces might, in part, be our society's overcommitment to organized sport for children and the many ways that commitment creates stress and drains energy that could otherwise be directed to fostering healthy familial relationships.

Recently, though, academics have called for research into this more detrimental aspect of the contemporary family's overcommitment to organized sports. According to Statistics Canada, in 2005, fifty-one percent of Canadian children ages five to fourteen participated in organized athletics. The *Livestrong* website puts the American number higher (sixty-nine percent for girls and seventy-five percent for boys). Many academics and journalists and educators have written about the concerning decline in this number (and the related concerns of inactivity and obesity), but given that over half of North American families continue to be involved in organized sport, the effect that commitment has on the family also bears exploration. In a 2016 essay, Matthew D. Johnson, director of the marriage and family studies laboratory at Binghamton University, argues that people with kids are less likely to be happy but more likely to stay married — a double bind that rings true with me. After reviewing thirty years of research studies, Johnson concludes that most romantic relationships do decline over time, but those relationships deteriorate notably faster for those tasked with parenting. Johnson cites an eight-year prospective study in which Brian D. Doss and his colleagues drew on data from 218 couples to conclude that the decline in relationship satisfaction is nearly twice as sharp in couples who have children than in childless couples. Johnson dismisses the idea that "kids will bring us closer" as a myth. Instead, lovers turn into parents. Recently, academics have begun to posit that the shift becomes even more dramatic when a child in the family takes up competitive sports and thereby dictates the schedule of the entire household. In "Understanding How Organized Youth Sport May Be Harming Individual Players within the Family Unit," Corliss Bean and her colleagues argue that organized sport puts a serious strain on marital relationships, and parents only begin to regain their relationship once the children finish sport or can manage it on their own as adults.

In other words, if I can hold on, Marty and I might start to get back what we once had. I need to wait only another ten years or so. One more decade.

I don't think I can do it.

I feel the truth of that loss of togetherness, the truth of lovers turned to parents, all the long, snowy drive to Creston, feel it like a burning lump of coal in the pit of my stomach. I want Marty to be nice. I want Marty to disappear. I don't know what I want. I want things to be different. I miss fun. I miss kissing.

I miss passion and urgency too.

I'm not talking about married sex — loading the dishwasher, brushing our teeth, turning out the lights, crawling under the covers, and then rolling toward each other out of habit. I'm talking about not being able to keep our hands off each other, tearing at clothes, not even making it to the bed. I'm talking about bite marks and bruises and animal sounds. I miss that.

Melissa, a hockey-mom friend, confided to me that married sex doesn't interest her: "Missionary position between paying the bills and folding the laundry, no thanks. I want a man to throw me against the wall." I wouldn't have thought it of her. If I'd taken the time to imagine her sex life, I would've pictured missionary position after the laundry. She's the kind of woman who packs healthy lunches, schedules homework hour for after school, and never misses a free educational opportunity at the local library. I quote her confession, anonymously but often. *"Can you believe it?!"* I'm astonished to hear such a clear expression of desire from someone who — like me — lives an ordinary life of an ordinary middle-aged mother. Fifty-year-old mothers of two do not typically admit to missing fucking. They're not supposed to want a man who will push them up against a wall in a fit of passion.

Last summer over margaritas, I complained to Marty and his college roommate (our UWO swimming teammate JT) that part of my sexual life had reached its end. "It came to me only now. I will never again have sex with someone new. I will not have that feeling of getting to know someone and realizing that I *like* him and then that he *likes* me too, that excitement of taking off each other's clothes for the first time. I don't know why I had this realization ten years into marriage, but it hit me like a death sentence. I pictured myself standing in a grave, up to my waist. *Just bury me now! Get it over with!*"

We were into some tequila and I could talk with this openness. Marty and JT laughed too. "Men have that epiphany at the altar," JT told me. "We're looking deep in your eyes and saying *I do*, but we're thinking *fuuuuuuuuuck.*"

Even on these good nights, we make fun of our marriages, of our sex lives. We've become something we never imagined: typical middle-aged parents. In a 2010 *Guardian* article, Amelia Hill argues that parents will raise happier kids if they put those kids second to their marriage. The idea makes me laugh. Kids second to marriage? Marty won't even put a three a.m. beer in his friend's garage second to our marriage. And, he would counter, I certainly do not put my career second to our marriage. No, our marriage comes dead last in a very long list of priorities. We act like our marriage will somehow take care of itself.

• • •

I let Ollie plug into his iPad for the trip to Creston. Normally I try to pull his attention away from the virtual world and toward the window.

"Look! A car in the ditch!"

"Look! Mountain goats!"

"Look! Windmills!"

"Look! The world!"

But today, I need the quiet time to put a lid on my emotions. A close friend once told me that the best time he spent with his children was while driving to sporting events. "It's perfect. They're trapped with you in a small space, side by side, for hours. They feel compelled to fill the silence, and because they don't have to look directly at you, they feel freer. They can be honest without feeling self-conscious. They say things shoulder-to-shoulder that they would never say while looking you in the eye at the kitchen table." I miss that small-space talk on this drive, but I get it at night in our shared hotel room, my favorite part of sport trips. A night owl with a busy mind, Ollie always struggles to fall asleep. In the dark with me at his side, he's more comfortable sharing his thoughts. We have the craziest, loveliest conversations.

"Mom, do you ever feel like your brain is not your own? Like other people are always telling you what you have to do and think?"

"Mom, do you ever wish you were a wolf and could live in the wilderness without any rules?"

His nine-year-old thoughts remind me of a younger Ollie. At four as he lay wide awake long before sunrise, I told him to close his eyes and *please please please* go to sleep, and he replied, "But I like sleeping with my eyes open so I can watch my dreams clucking by." At six he asked me why there weren't any aunt brothers. To my confusion, he replied, "People are always talking about great writings of our aunt sisters. Didn't men do any of the great writings? Weren't there any aunt *brothers*?"

Ancestors, he meant. I always thought I'd remember every wild word Ollie spoke. Now I know: I forget. In light of the other things that seem to have come and gone lately, I feel this forgetting too intensely. Over the weekend, I scribble Ollie's sentences in a little notebook. I'll remember them all. I know that if he saw my pages full of Ollie quotations, he would find me embarrassing. I find me embarrassing.

Dr. Madeline Levine claims that children of overly involved parents are three times more likely to suffer depression and anxiety. Hitting a little too close to my heart, she argues that such devotion is often a thinly disguised attempt of parents to correct what did not go right in their own childhoods. Levine casts yet another vote for redirecting a significant portion of our parenting energy back toward our marriages.

There are so many ways for parents to screw up.

• • •

The first game against Nelson is ridiculously rough, and I can't say I'm getting used to it. I watch through barely opened fingers. Quinn, one of our best but roughest players, spends most of the game in the penalty box. I tell Roland the story about my discovery in the Innsbruck museum: a statue of a peasant with the same last name as Quinn. This potential ancestor led the Austrian peasants in revolt against Napoleon and won! "That great-great-great-uncle of Quinn would've spent a lot of time in the penalty box too," I laugh. I tell Quinn he's descended from Austrian warriors. Already my European trip fades. I want to hold onto that Angie, the competent one. My marriage, more than anything else, makes me feel incompetent.

Messages come in from the Fernie ski hill, the tone conciliatory. Normally, I would send a play-by-play of each game, letting Marty know every move Ollie made, but I can't shake today's anger. I pull up Marty's contact information and block him. There: that's easy. I turn my attention back to the hockey.

I immerse myself in the sounds and smells of the rink. It's early enough in the season that I'm not sick of the rink yet. It still invokes nostalgic feelings associated with my own youth. I know that will change. Last year near the end of the season when

I couldn't stand one more minute in the rink, I had one of my brilliant brainstorms. One building over from the arena stands Fernie's Park Place Lodge. Inside the hotel, there happens to be a hotel bar, one that used to go by the utilitarian name of The Pub. When I first came to Fernie to visit Marty in 1996, he and all of his cute friends bartended there. After last call, the manager kicked everyone else out, and I stayed with the attentive boys, drinking and playing pool until the sun rose. Back then Fernie was a hardcore ski town that attracted few women. The woman-to-man ratio made me a popular visitor, always. Darcy, Tyler, Trevor, Mike — all of them gave me their full attention. On that first night at The Pub, sometime around three a.m., the manager emptied the lost-and-found and gave each of us a pair of ski gloves to take home. "Free (G)love Night at The Pub," he announced joyfully. Fernie was odd like that. None of us had kids or careers or any reason to fret about the hangovers we were working hard to deserve.

Nostalgic for those days of no responsibility, I had the late-season brainstorm: I should drop Ollie off at the rink and instead of watching practice, I could mosey over to The Pub. Maybe someone I knew would be there. I could have a beer and zip back before Ollie even knew I'd gone.

I felt silly walking through those double-swinging doors to the smell of beer-soaked carpets. My eyes had to adjust to the dark. What kind of mom would ditch her kid at practice and go for beer?

But then I looked to the bar and who sat there?

Darcy! Tyler! Kieran! Jay!

Stupidly happy, I grinned at them all. I felt like I'd strolled straight into 1996.

One by one, they turned my way, equally happy to see me.

All but Jay who hadn't liked me that much in 1996 and still didn't on this sudden reappearance. But even his grumpy non-acknowledgment of my arrival felt oddly nostalgic.

Tyler and Darcy — all charm — gave me the impression they'd been sitting there since 1996 just in case I came back. I felt twenty-seven years old, the pretty girl new to town.

We joked this beer would become my hockey night ritual. "Marty doesn't have to know," Tyler smiled, displaying the same deep dimples and mischievous eye glint that made him so popular two decades ago. A Millerville hockey player from way back, Tyler still had the magnetic confidence of all successful athletes. That kind of self-assurance sticks well after the player retires the skates.

"Totally our secret," Darcy agreed with a wink.

I hugged them both, again. "It's so great to see you guys."

Tyler insisted on paying for my pint, and I floated out of there. God that was fun. I felt younger, sexier, happier. A little flirting, a little laughing, a little attention — an easy boost.

When I got home, I did tell Marty about my side trip to The Pub. Still buzzing, more from the company than the beer, I said, "You should drive Ollie to practice one night. Then you just pop over to the Park Place and have a quick beer with your old buddies. The whole crew. It was so fun to see them. Still there, still the same."

"You went for beer while Ollie practiced?" Marty did not share my elevated mood or my enthusiasm for this latest brilliant idea.

"Well, yeah, but just one."

"Quality parenting, Ang."

"Marty, I didn't have to tell you at all. It was one beer with old friends. Fun, remember that? You should go. You could use some fun." As I turned away, I muttered words like surly, grumpy, annoying.

"Drinking while you drive your son to hockey? I would never do that."

And that's where Marty and I stand — the night of my quality parenting and my return from Austria are different parts of the same story. Neither of us can take a moment of pleasure without the other adding it to a long tally of resentment. I go to Austria:

121

point Marty. Marty goes to poker: point me. I enjoy a pint with old friends: point him. Who's the better parent? Who gives the kids more? Who cares more about the family? Who has a more rightful claim to utter exhaustion?

David Code, author of the bestselling book *To Raise Happy Kids, Put Your Marriage First*, claims "devoted parents do not produce happy children" and suggests instead of trying to be the perfect parent, we should try to be the perfect spouse. Ayelet Waldman words this suggestion more strongly. In *Bad Mother: A Chronicle of Maternal Crimes*, Waldman urges, "Love each other desperately, ardently, more than you love your children."

More than we love our children? Blasphemy! But Waldman calls for research that proves once and for all that parents who love each other intensely, who make a conscious decision to nurture their love for each other, will raise children who have successful and happy lives. Psychologists have, of course, extensively studied the effect that parental relationships have on the children. Donald Winnicott, for example, explains that a loving parental relationship creates a safe and protective environment for a child's self-discovery. Parents who genuinely love each other and openly show affection will positively shape their child's idea of self, create a predictable and nurturing space for growth, and provide a model for the child to foster healthy relationships in the future. Dr. Winnicott also stresses that only when parents have their emotional needs met do they become capable of meeting their children's needs. Ayelet Waldman needn't have issued a new call for research on ways in which parents' romantic love is good for their children. Winnicott's work dates back to the 1960s.

So, yes, a loving parental relationship improves a child's quality of life. I'm suspicious, though, of the extent to which I'm drawn to the extreme wording used by both David Code and Ayelet Waldman. The impossible quest for perfection — the perfect parent, the perfect spouse — is part of the same drive to excess that has poisoned youth sport. Instead, we should turn our focus to balance. Rather than loving our spouse more than our children — as Waldman urges — why not slow down enough that we have time and space to nurture love for everyone in our family, without making it a contest over who gets more? Fostering an affectionate and caring relationship with a spouse need not trump a loving relationship with our children. In less hectic lives, we can find energy for all these loves.

I'm susceptible to these ideas of perfection-in-love and love-as-contest for the same reason I sometimes fall into the *more! more! more!* mindset of competitive sport. I'm drawn to that intensity even though I know excessiveness does not lead to happiness or serenity. I grew up immersed in the world of high-level competition, a world that valued faster and stronger and better rather than happier and more serene. That high-pressure sporting mindset affects my attitude toward everything: my career, my children, my recreation, my marriage. The work of cultural commentators like David Code and Ayelet Waldman suggests that I am not alone in this tendency to excess and imbalance.

I kept going to The Pub and meeting the guys. Not every week but every month or two. Whenever I needed a lift. I knew I could count on Tyler and Darcy. Their smiling *Angie!* as I came through the swinging doors would boost me through another stretch of the parenting tedium Marty and I had fallen into. It assured me that 1996 Angie — the fun Angie, the likable Angie, the sexy Angie — still existed in me somewhere. Tyler and Darcy could see her. I quit telling Marty about my visits to The Pub, but sometimes, during an especially snarky transition from dinner to hockey practice, as I headed to the car with Ollie and his gear, I'd hear Marty's falsely sing-song voice, "Say hi to Tyler and the boys!"

· · ·

On this Creston trip, I feel sad about my fight with Marty, and I use Ollie's picky eating as an excuse to separate myself from the group. I don't want to socialize. When everyone else gathers for pierogis at a highly recommended diner, Ollie and I grab some cheeseburgers at the Dairy Queen drive-through and retreat to our room. He lets me read Percy Jackson to him, though he has long preferred reading to himself. Unfairly, I've tied my hopes of happiness to him this weekend, and he knows it. He does what he can to help.

Both my kids tend to fatten up before they gain height. They grow out and then up. Ollie must have an up-phase coming. Even his wrists have a little roll around them, reminding me of pudgy baby Ollie. I loop my index finger and thumb around his wrist as I read, and because I don't say anything about the baby fat, he lets me. If I stay quiet, I can hold onto him, for now.

As I turn the pages, my eyes flash to my iPhone out of habit. But Marty remains blocked and my phone remains quiet. I think again of Grandma Jean and her advice to never go to bed without resolving a dispute. What would she think of me here in a dingy hotel room, eating greasy cheeseburgers, and refusing to answer my husband's calls? Knowing what we should do in marriage does not necessitate doing it.

We do try, though, sometimes. Last summer we initiated a weekly date night. Those always give way to the schedule once we head into fall, but the simple practice of regular dates does tend to work while it lasts. In late August, Marty and I tackled an adrenaline-fueled bike ride on the mountain trails above our house and then lounged in the sun on a downtown patio, enjoying a beer. Marty looked handsome sitting across from me in a tank top, his arms golden in the perfect evening light. My quads throbbed, pleasantly fatigued, and I slid into a state of relaxation I feel only after intense exercise (or intense orgasm). With the sun still warm on my skin and a cold beer in my hand, I felt comfortable admitting that I'd overextended myself in recent years and that those commitments might account for some of our marital challenges. "Stress is toxic," I said, feeling momentarily free of it. "And we both carry too much of it, stress and toxicity. I could make changes to curb mine." He nodded, afraid of some criticism coming his way. But I would surprise him. I felt generous on the high of post-ride endorphins. "After I finish this novel," I said, "I'm going to take a break from writing. A couple of years maybe. I just won't write another book until the kids are —"

What the fuck was he fiddling with? I followed the downward cast of his eyes and saw he had his iPhone under the table, thumbs tapping madly. My good mood, my eagerness to admit my culpability, my keenness to make change — *Poof!* Gone. Could Marty not understand that I was trying to tell him something important? Was this really the time to be playing with his damn phone?

"Could you listen to me for one second?" I snapped. "I'm trying to —"

"There! Got it!" Marty flashed me his iPhone screen and a smile, as he pressed a big round button with his thumb. "Can you say that again?"

He'd been trying to record my promise.

"After this novel," I repeated slowly, "I will not write another book for two years. I will take a break. I will enjoy my children."

"Got it!" He said, pressing *pause*. The smile that wooed me back in 1995 filled his face. "That's legally binding, I think. It's recorded."

We both laughed.

I, of course, did not take a hiatus from writing. I broke my promise, as Marty knew I would. But he's done nothing to push back on his stress either. We tell ourselves we can't, but we're making a choice. Every year we choose to take on more. We do not make this parenting thing easy on ourselves.

When I first met Marty, I had the inconvenient situation of being married to someone else. While that first marriage fell apart, I approached the problem like any graduate student would: research, research, research! I read every philosophy book I could

125

find on love and sex and marriage. My favorite theory goes like this: love is essentially narcissistic. We fall in love not so much with the other person as with our own image reflected in that person's eyes. In 1995, the "me" I saw in my first husband's eyes had issues: hard to please, demanding, too many goals, unrealistic goals, too scattered, too anxious, too much. Then I met Marty on the varsity swim team, and I very much preferred the image I saw reflected in his eyes: fit, fast, and fun.

More than twenty years later, what do I see when I look at myself through Marty's eyes? A nagging shrew.

I hate to think what he sees in the mirror I hold up to him: someone who always falls short, who's never enough, who constantly disappoints.

I wish marriage didn't tug people so hard in this direction: the euphoria of new love inevitably followed by the tedium of commitment and shared responsibility. In the words of Matthew D. Johnson, "the course of true love runs downhill."

But I could take steps to slow this downward course. I could show Marty a better Marty. He's a great dad. Katie adores him. Ollie wants to be him. I married a ski bum who morphed into a senior lead at a successful company. Marty has, unexpectedly, turned out to be an excellent provider. I could praise him for our comfortable lifestyle. I never do. And, on our good days, nobody makes me laugh like Marty makes me laugh. He works wonders with a Crock-Pot. He still swims a melt-my-heart gorgeous butterfly. But none of these strengths appear in the reflection I show him.

Why?

Because I'm too mad about where he leaves the laundry?

Because I'm hurt that poker night excited his interest more than my return from Austria?

We've chosen *Have fun! Try hard!* as our family motto, but when it comes to marriage we're doing neither.

• • •

On the drive home from Creston, Ollie babbles about the weekend. He likes the story part of sport the best. We'll be reliving this tournament until the next one, but his narrative always sits at odds with everyone else's version of the weekend. The Fernie Ghostriders didn't win a single game, but in his tale their team somehow emerges victorious. He rattles on about refereeing errors and miscounted goals and some complicated scoring system that only he understands. He's young. I let him revel in his delusion. The snow keeps falling. I grip the wheel hard and stick between the two white lines, barely visible. I bet Marty and Katie had a great weekend in all this powder. I don't know for sure because I still have Marty blocked. But I'm almost at a point where I can laugh at my ridiculous tantrum. I have blocked my own husband?

I glance down at my iPhone on the console and see a new message has popped up from a male academic friend. The opening lines read, "Before you read this email: don't worry. None of it will affect you or your family —"

Uh-oh. I pull over to the side of the highway and read the rest.

"Just hold on, Ollie. I've got a work email to answer." My heart has stopped pounding all together. My blood feels heavy in my arms. I take a deep breath. Something bad has happened.

I mentioned that I think of "Angie Abdou, the writer" as someone different than "Mom." I've taken that separation a little far lately. Over the last year, I've struck up a flirtation with an American colleague. Let's call him Thomas. Offline, Thomas and I have been in each other's company only a handful of times. But I love the way he looks at me. He makes me feel twenty-seven. I get so caught up in this sexy version of myself that when I walk by a mirror and catch a glimpse of my true reflection, it's alarming. *Oh my god! What happened to my face?!* Because I am not twenty-seven. I am forty-seven. Married with two children. But in my exchanges with Thomas, I pretend otherwise. I like this little make-believe, the reprieve from regular life. I had been thinking of it as a thing apart, something that does not touch my true life.

However, the email tells me his wife has gotten wind of our inappropriate connection. "We have to cut off our correspondence and should not see each other again."

I'd invited Thomas to participate on a sport literature panel with me in Lethbridge next month. When I think of that trip, I feel like a lovesick teenager. I want him to come. The email cancels the trip. We will not be seeing each other again. He would like me to email once more to let him know I'm okay with this news, and then we must break off all contact.

I should be worried about his canceled participation. I've scheduled the panel for January, less than a month away. I've enticed audiences, paid for air tickets, won grants, and distributed posters. That's what should concern me, the professional implications. But all I can think is: *He's not coming? I want him to come!*

I swear under my breath, sigh, and pull back on the snowy highway.

"You okay, Mom?"

"Yep. Just a work email."

"Do you think we got six goals and not four in that second game?"

"I do think so, Ollie."

"Did you see me get off the ice in the middle of that shift? It's because I poked a guy on the other team right here with my stick." He points at his breastbone. "The ref didn't see it. I felt bad."

"It's not a big deal, Ollie. Kids get poked in hockey." Even as I say it, I wonder again what we're trying to teach kids through this sport. Not the value of a kind and cooperative society. Not empathy.

"But he was crying on the bench. I saw him!"

"It's okay, Ollie." I've got no energy for these assurances. It's not okay to hurt people, even accidentally.

Ollie senses my lack of engagement and goes quiet.

At home, Marty's trademark grin welcomes us. In that smile, I always see a much younger Marty. I keep a photograph of him

128

at thirty-two after he and I bushwhacked our way up a mountain to find a rumored cave. He stands in the cave's mouth with his hands above his head, victorious. When his mom saw the photo she laughed, "That smile! He looks sixteen. Will he ever grow up?"

"I hope not," I replied.

It was the first thing I noticed about him when we met: the smile and then the abs and then his beautiful butterfly and then his warm hands. "Oh, here you are," I say. "I thought I blocked you."

We laugh. I've blocked him before. Real life is not that easy. He puts up with me.

As always, he initiates the hug. I gratefully receive it. "You all right?" He steps back, studying my face. I smile and lean back into the hug, hoping he won't notice I've been crying.

"Yes," I lie. "I'm fine. I'll just grab Ollie's hockey stuff from the trunk." Later I will get defensive and project blame. I would not be so intrigued by another man if my own relationship gave me what I need. But not now. Now I feel like a schmuck. I had somehow convinced myself that the flirtation with Thomas had nothing to do with Marty. A thing apart. A little treat, just for me. For "Angie Abdou, the writer," not for "Mom." Definitely not for "Wife." But now my secret friend Thomas is here in the room with me and Ollie and Katie and Marty, even if only I know. *I'm sorry, Marty.* "I'm totally all right," I say again and retreat to the garage. I wipe a sleeve hard across my eyes as I leave.

CHAPTER SEVEN

HOME ICE
HOCKEY HOLIDAY!

I mope for a few days. Marty doesn't notice. We live largely separate lives. Ice at the rink. Ice at home. We've taken the divide-and-conquer approach of sport parents too far. I wonder if we can bridge the divide when hockey and ski seasons come to an end, but for now I'm relieved the chasm allows me to sort through my emotions without having to answer to my husband.

It's not like I've never had a crush before. Marty's well aware of my writer crushes. He always pronounces Steve Heighton's name in breathless ecstasy: "SteeeeevEN! HeighhhhhTON!"

"Marty! Stop it!"

"What?! That's the way *you* say it. I thought maybe he was Swedish or something."

Two years ago, Marty (keeping tabs on me via Twitter) discovered that I'd instigated a leg-wrestling competition in a festival hospitality suite. When I returned home, Marty asked, "Okay, who were you leg-wrestling with?"

"Trevor Cole and Joseph Boyden."

"Fuck, Angie. Seriously." That was Marty's only response.

When I quoted him, Trevor said, "But surely your husband *knows* you, right?" Yep, he knows me. Hence the succinct response.

But Thomas is different. His name would mean nothing to Marty. I haven't sighed a word of Thomas's existence. Why not? Because this flirtation feels not so harmless? Because my thirst for attention has put me a single misstep away from jeopardizing my home and complicating my children's lives? Because I'm so very tired of being a grown-up?

Time zips along, oblivious to my inner crisis. I mourn a relationship that existed mostly in my imagination. It fits that the grief should take place in the same realm, invisible to the solid people moving about in my real life. Ollie turns ten, and I throw him a party with way too many boys. They fill the hot tub — hockey-player soup — throwing themselves from the scorching water into huge snowbanks. I never knew humans could be so loud, high on the thrill of being alive. When I let them inside, they tear apart the house like only a pack of boys can. Nobody would look at Ollie and think: anxious or antisocial or oversensitive or odd. He's as wild as the rest of his team, so fully immersed in happy destruction that even he doesn't notice my new mood. I'm grateful for the reprieve from his worried *Are you okay, Mom? Are you okay? Are you sure you're okay?*

I'm not okay, but my well-being should not be the concern of my ten-year-old boy.

Messages come in from Thomas. Or at least from his email account. His tone has changed. These notes sound nothing like the Thomas I have come to know. Each message makes me sadder.

I suspect he writes them with heavy guidance from his wife. He plural pronouns me to death: *we think, we've decided, we feel it would best if, my partner and I will be spending some time . . .*

His partner has been very forgiving, he tells me.

There's no *we* on my end of the email exchange. I'm alone with these developments, only me and a hot tub full of rowdy hockey boys.

I do write Thomas a few times, despite his clear instructions that I should not. He flat-out told me to respond once, to let him know how I was doing with this news, and then to disappear. But my emotions do not obey. Like these reveling birthday boys, my feelings run wild, uncontrollable, potentially destructive.

In response to each of my messages, Thomas dismisses me again.

We're working hard on this end.

It has nothing to do with you.

His subtext is clear: *please go away.*

He saturates his messages with a New Age sentiment I would not have associated with him. He's working on mindfulness, on being present. He and his partner have been in deep and trans-formative conversation every day. He's advancing, evolving. He's dealing with past demons. He will not attempt to put this very important work into words for fear of getting it wrong.

I imagine his wife reading over his shoulder and think: I *bet* you're afraid of getting it wrong.

Anger begins to replace my sadness. I swear that if I get one more of these ridiculous letters written in his wife's sentences, I will publicly retract every kind thing I have ever said about his work and his intellect.

But I can't hold on to that anger. Boredom and tedium and loneliness in my home have turned into real trouble in his home. I've caused him (and his wife) that distress, and here I am, getting off consequence-free. Marty has no clue.

Plus, I sense a hidden message in the *go away* subtext of these emails. I read: *calm down, let me sort things out, and maybe I can still come see you in January.*

So I do go away. In response, I get a note: *We have decided to keep my commitment to the scheduled event. We do not make this decision for my work or for the audience, but for the three of us. We think it would be best if you and I can see each other and find a way to settle upon a simple friendship. We both extend a wish that you can be present for your family at Christmas.*

I hate that we.

But a simple friendship? I will take it.

• • •

I make a decision to step right out of this sadness, this anxiety. I embrace the holiday season. I bop around the house, wrapping presents, decorating the tree, sipping eggnog. I even sing Christmas carols. I never sing, especially Christmas carols.

In *Midnight Hockey*, Bill Gaston says hockey players are good at the game of life because they "know how to play hurt." Maybe that's true of all athletes. This Christmas season, I play hurt. Nobody notices.

"What has gotten into you?" Marty asks. "You're positively jolly."

"It's Christmas," I chirp. "I love Christmas!"

"No, you don't. You hate Christmas."

"Not this year. This year I love it!"

Marty's skeptical, but he goes along with me. Everyone prefers happy Angie.

After a few days, that happiness starts to feel genuine. Over the Christmas break, I rediscover my family, my home. It feels good to settle in, to be here without wishing myself elsewhere, to inhabit my family life fully, without worrying what that presence costs my other lives. I take some time off work. We're on a hockey break too, and it turns out that I have a daughter!

Why hello, Katie. Nice to meet you. You're a lovely little creature.

133

A true artist with an eye for beauty, sparkly beauty in particular, Katie loves the tree ornaments. She and I spend two evenings shoulder-to-shoulder, picking the best ones and finding the perfect branch for each. Our tree, thanks to Katie, becomes a work of creative genius.

Katie's long list of future careers includes fashion designer, and she pulls together some fabulous outfits for the Christmas season: snowflakes, candy canes, snowmen, Christmas trees — she wears them all and designs her jewelry to match. I have not let her pierce her ears, but inspired by the hanging tree decorations, she loops shiny baubles around her ears, so the jewels hang down by her lobes. She's gleeful at her cunning sidestep of my no-earring rule. Like the tree, Katie too becomes a work of creative genius.

I love watching my daughter, her shoulders back, her chin high, standing proud in her outlandish outfits and dangling earrings. I wish I could take a small piece of her confidence for myself.

I know credit for Katie's self-assurance goes straight to Marty. She believes in the Katie she sees reflected in her adoring father's eyes.

• • •

Like many contemporary families, we do not treat Christmas as a religious holiday. On my side of the family, Ollie and Katie sit a few generations away from religion. In my childhood, Sundays meant not God but sport. We spent weekends at wrestling tournaments and swim meets and hockey games. Religion played a big role in Marty's childhood, though. His maternal grandfather was an Anglican minister in South Africa. After moving from South Africa to Canada, Marty served as an altar boy throughout his youth in Ontario. Later, in Fernie, Marty's father led the church choir, and Marty's mom produced the church newsletter.

On Marty's side of the family, Ollie and Katie are first-generation no church. Marty's relatively recent step away from organized religion was conscious. Early in our relationship, he chose science over God and mountain sports over church. Struck by a comedian who mocked agnosticism as a feeble-minded copout, Marty decided on the spot: there is no God. Since Marty has always had a low tolerance for grey areas, Marty-as-atheist makes good sense. Even if I'm not willing to join him, I do understand him. Any Sunday, you can find him hiking the trails above our house or straight-lining the black-diamond runs at Fernie Alpine Resort, "testing the edge of control," he tells me.

Even before life as parents, we had chosen sport over organized religion, spending our Sunday mornings getting fresh tracks at the local ski hill or road-tripping to Alberta to compete in Masters swim meets. Church plays no role at all in the lives of our children, and they know no different. Before Ollie turned four, his great-grandmother Jean died, long predeceased by her Anglican minster husband. GG's funeral was the first time Ollie set tiny foot in a church.

Marty and I sat in the front pew, trying our best to keep baby Katie and toddler Ollie respectfully quiet. We did a passable job until the minister entered in a long white robe trimmed in black and gold. Ollie took one look at the minister's colors and asked in a "whisper" that could be heard clear to the back pew: "DOES THAT GUY PLAY FOR THE BRUINS?"

Sport had clearly eclipsed religion in Ollie's childhood, just as it had in my childhood. Academic writers have spilled much ink on the topic of sport as religion, coming up with phrases like "alternative forms of the sacred," "civic religion," and "reconceptualizing sport as sacred phenomenon." Mostly they're talking about sport fandom as a replacement for the ritual and community of organized religion. In a 2010 *Psychology Today* article called "Why Atheism Will Replace Religion," for example, Nigel Barber notes that sports spectatorship provides much the same kind of social and spiritual benefits as people obtain from church. His argument draws on *Sport Fans: The Psychology and Social Impact of Spectators*, a 2001 book by Daniel Wann et al. Wann and his co-authors note that sport fandom and religious practices share the same vocabulary: faith, devotion, worship, ritual, dedication, sacrifice, commitment, spirit, prayer, and suffering. They argue that sport arenas exist synonymously with "cathedrals where followers gather to worship their heroes and pray for their successes." Many scholars agree, easily citing examples of the way sport has usurped religion: group mentality, ritualistic chants, worship of heroes, and a link between devotion and violence.

In Canada, hockey fans in particular demonstrate a religious fervor for their game of choice. During the 2010 Vancouver Olympics, American commentators repeatedly referred to hockey as Canada's religion. In a *Vancouver Sun* article, Douglas Todd concedes that, though the association between Canadian hockey and Canadian religion might be unoriginal and overused, "there is a lot of truth to it," and in Canada, "hockey is a very powerful civil religion." Todd explains that the phrase "civil religion" was made famous in the 1970s by sociologist Robert Bellah, who used the term to refer to "any set of beliefs and rituals related to the past, present, and/or future of a people ('nation') giving that people a transcendent sense of their collective destiny." In worship of a team and devotion to its players, fans unite. If they can collectively cheer loud enough, or pray hard enough, they imagine redemption and salvation in their team's future victories. Wearing the right colors tells those fans who they are, what they're hoping for, and what imagined future they're moving toward.

Think of Habs fans with their worship of "Jesus Price." It's easy to see the parallels between sport fandom and religious fervor, but I wonder if the same might be true of the *practice* of sport. Can playing sport also fill some of the needs traditionally met by organized religion? Hockey gives structure to life. Players show up every day at the same time and ritualistically move through the sets of drills. As with a church service, participants come to know exactly how the hour of devotion will be structured (warm-up, drills, scrimmage, team talk, cheer), and players of all ages look to the coach for guidance the way parishioners look to the pastor. Sport thereby imposes meaning on a life. The players train hard, suffering and sacrificing themselves in the now for results in the future. They also learn to downplay the desires of the individual in favor of a greater good for the whole, stressing belonging and community as central to their identity in a way similar to church-goers.

When faced with parenting, we decided that we'd tell Ollie and Katie about all religions and let them make their own decisions. When they ask about death or souls or heaven or gods, we always start our answer with "Well, some people believe . . ." In the second part of the sentence, we aim primarily for variety. I put my university courses in religious studies to work and compose answers ranging from Christian to Hindu to Jewish to Buddhist to Zoroastrian to agnostic to Baha'i to atheist. Marty and I give our children the information, and the children decide for themselves what to believe.

I thought this plan very clever until the day I heard five-year-old Ollie tell his three-year-old sister, "When you die, you get to see god and if you've been bad, he sends you to hell, but if you've been good, he lets you decide what animal you're going to be in your next life."

Religion fusion.

Last year, Ollie developed a fascination with Rick Riordan's Percy Jackson series, wherein a select group of eleven-year-olds discover the reason they're odd, the reason they don't quite fit in, is because they're descended from Greek and Roman gods. More recently, I overheard seven-year-old Katie tell a grade-one classmate, "I don't like going to summer camps where they try to tell you what to believe, like Christian or whatever. I think you can believe whatever you want to believe. Like my brother, he believes Greek."

I know Ollie secretly hopes he *is* a demigod and that the explanation for his own weirdness can be found in his divine parentage and that soon his own supernatural gifts will be clear to everyone. If he had his pick, he'd be like Percy, a son of Poseidon. I try to convince him that as a potential son of Poseidon, he might prefer a swim club to the hockey team.

The team sport of swimming filled that church space for me and Marty in our twenties, giving us a community and telling us who we were and where we should be, as well as hinting at how our future might look, if we dedicated ourselves as we should. Our relationship with nature, fostered through our outdoor sports, also filled spiritual needs that might otherwise have been met by religion. And there is even something spiritual about the mind frame reached in sport practice at its best, that ideal state anthropologists call "flow" — a state of such exertion and focus that athletes transcend place and time and self. In flow, the mind quiets and the athlete becomes unaware of performing for an audience. The outside world vanishes. The chattering stops. This experience of no-mindness is similar to the Zen state of mind as practiced in Buddhism.

I found my own religion on the bottom of a swimming pool, in the meditative back and forth, morning and night, in the community of my swim team, in the sense of purpose provided by attendance records and grueling workouts and time standards. Sport practice, then, can work at a deep, spiritual level where sport fandom works at a surface, ritualistic one. Swimming gave my life meaning in the daily work, in the dedicated quest to long-term goals and in the rewards of competition as well as the disappointments. Sport mirrors religion in the way it imposes a story — a narrative structure — on the random chaos of real life. At ten, Ollie has only begun to sort out where he finds that kind of meaning and belonging, but so far it's partly through the sense of acceptance he gets as a member of the Atom Fernie Ghostriders' community.

• • •

So in our home, Christmas is secular, a homage to family rather than traditional religion. For us, Christmas Day means skiing. We get to the hill early, and all four of us *woot!* our way down wide open runs, never waiting in a single lift line, while other families linger over gifts and coffee with Baileys.

Katie's skiing has improved dramatically. Only seven years old, she flies down the intermediate runs, fast on her big brother's heels. I race behind her, screaming "KATIE! SLOW DOWN!" Where did this rad chick come from? Last time I skied with my family, I had a snow-plowing little girl. I watch her death-defying antics and realize how much I miss while I'm on the road with hockey. In a literature review summarizing the oft-ignored detrimental effects of organized youth sport, Corliss Bean and her colleagues include "neglect of the sibling." It's true. While I do everything I can to facilitate Ollie's participation in his sport of choice, I have, on weekends at least, left the rearing of Katie to her dad. I envy their tight father-daughter bond, but Marty has earned it. Katie's face lights up with love every time she looks at him. He's her Dee-Da and she's his KK. When they meet eyes, nobody else exists.

Despite my harsh judgment of my dad, and my disappointment at his absentee parenting style, I expect I might eventually owe Katie the same apology. I haven't watched one of her skiing races ever. I'm always gone to hockey. With my commitment to that sport's travel, I can no longer bring myself to invest the thousand dollars for a season's ski pass, which means I hardly get up to the hill anymore. Marty jumps into that role. He sends me the videos of his speed demon. I watch them at the rink. We need a better parenting strategy. Soon. I hope Katie isn't as slow to forgive me as I have been to forgive my father.

In the car on the way home from the last tournament before Christmas, I wondered aloud how Katie's ski tournament had gone and Ollie told me, "I'm kind of like your kid, and Katie's kind of like dad's kid." Ollie accepts that Marty misses most of his hockey games, but he thinks it fair that I should miss Katie's races in exchange.

Katie rarely complains about the lack of maternal involvement in her sporting life, not yet. But when she's overtired, her strong exterior cracks. She's tired a lot over Christmas. Late at night when she should be sleeping, she calls me to her room. "Why do you like Ollie better than me?"

"I don't. I couldn't like anyone better than I like you." I tuck a curl behind her ear. Her bright red hair surprised me at her birth. I'd already had one child and thought I had a clear idea what my children looked like — like my brother and my dad. I didn't expect this fair-skinned, regal child. Marty and I had picked all kinds of zippy names for her — Zoe or Zadie or Lizzy. But she came into the world looking like a medieval queen. We waited three days before we settled on the classic Katherine Elizabeth.

It's true: I could not like anyone more than I like her.

"You *act* like you love Ollie more than you love me." She rolls on her side, her curls splaying across her pink pillowcase, her freckled face impossibly serious. She fixes her blue eyes hard on me, waiting for her answer. I look around her cluttered room once, picking my words carefully. She's packed the space with trinkets and dolls and costumes and board games and crafting supplies and jewelry and face paints. Like her dad, Katie loves to shop. The plastic mess gives me heart palpitations. I don't know how she sleeps in the middle of this nonbiodegradable chaos. Ollie, like me, keeps his room spare, nearly empty except for his overflowing bookcase. I remember his pride when I installed those shelves. "I've come up with a system," he told me, "and I don't want to brag, but I think it's pretty good." I thought maybe he'd organized his books alphabetically or by color or by genre. But no. The books he *likes* go on the bottom shelf, the ones he *really likes* go on the middle shelf, and the books he *likes the very most* go on the top shelf. Ollie organizes his books by love.

"I love you both," I tell Katie now. "I love you and your

140

brother exactly the same. But," I lower my voice and lean toward her ear, "I *worry* about Ollie more." I watch the little sister absorb this confession, ponder it. She's seen her big brother's sensitivity, his anxiety, his stress. Even at her young age, she has talked him down and protected him.

Katie gives one quick nod of comprehension, pursing her mouth in a tight line of resolve. She's strong because I ask it of her.

"You're my easy kid, KK." I kiss her in the middle of her fair forehead.

"Easy peasy lemon squeezy!" She sings it in an outburst of energy and cheerfulness, a dimple digging deep in her freckly cheek. I ask Katie to be easy, and so she is easy. She becomes what I need her to be. It's not fair, I know it.

• • •

Katie has recently expressed an interest in playing hockey, and in light of this late-night request for more love, I wonder if maybe she associates hockey with me and my attention. I do, after all, spend the bulk of my non-working time at the arena. Marty and I had hoped we'd avoid the hockey request from her. Many families have multiple kids in hockey, in different leagues, but Marty has no interest in doing the rink run and I can be in only one place at a time. Life would be so much less difficult if Katie stuck with skiing. Many of Katie's girlfriends have begun playing hockey, though. Where hockey numbers have generally declined, the number of girl hockey players increases every year. In Canada, 8,146 girls played in the 1990–91 season, 54,563 in 2001–02, and 85,624 in 2009–10. The rise in girl players is similar in the USA, leading American national team member Hilary Knight to declare our age "a critical time" for the growth of female hockey. Three girls play on Ollie's hockey team. The boys accept these girls without question, and, besides their pink helmets, they blend right in.

For now.

But I don't see a future in hockey for these Fernie girls. By Atom, the girls have their own change room and often get left out of pre-game and post-game instruction. They also miss out on the celebration and camaraderie and the treats. It's easy to forget them, quarantined in their separate quarters. I've poked my head into the female dressing room after a hockey game. It's a lonely place, made lonelier by the revelry happening right next door. By Pee Wee (ages eleven and twelve), female involvement in Fernie hockey has already dwindled to zero. The girls committed to continuing in the sport choose to play for an all-girl team in Cranbrook, which means driving one hundred kilometers each way for every practice. Mountain road conditions don't make that commitment appealing or sustainable. By high school, these girls drop out in favor of more accessible school sports like volleyball or basketball.

In 2012, I was invited to the World Women's Hockey Championships in Vermont to speak on a panel about sport and gender. I was the sport novelist on a panel of impressive athletes. The women spoke of how hard they fought to play this sport. Early female hockey players struggled against sexism of parents, coaches, and players to persevere in the leagues and gain legitimacy for women's hockey. In 2007, they established their own professional league, the Canadian Women's Hockey League (CWHL). In 2010, the league expanded into the United States and then into China in 2017. In Vermont, the women's passion for their sport inspired me. I was invigorated by their fierceness in refusing to take no for an answer and their relentless fight to dig out a space for themselves in this sport. But I also saw their weariness. Their passion for the game of hockey was matched by their frustration at the persistent sexism in sport culture. The CWHL started paying its players only in 2017. It pays each player $2,000 to $10,000 per year, with a team cap of $100,000. A rival league — the American NWHL — was established in 2015 and caps its salaries at a team total of $270,000 U.S. In 2017, NHL player Shea Weber collected a salary of fourteen million dollars. The average NHL salary in 2017? Four million dollars. The average NHL player makes fifteen times the entire team cap in the NWHL.

Clearly, women hockey players don't play the game for money or fame. They compete for love of hockey alone. That's what I admired about the female athletes I met in Vermont.

That's what I see too in the second-year Atom girls here in Fernie. I watch them on the ice, and god they're having fun — flying across the ice, roughhousing with the boys. Hockey wasn't an option for girls during my childhood, but I would've liked it, maybe for the same reasons Ollie does: heightened drama, real battle. But I'd also like it for other reasons: a place to stretch outside of traditional gender roles. I marvel at how quickly these gender restrictions have dissolved for this age group. I look forward to watching the barriers to women's hockey continue to fall. Having had a chance, in Vermont, to meet some of the fierce women at the helm, I'm confident that the sport will continue to move toward equality. As a feminist, I'm nothing but ecstatic about the growth in girls' hockey.

As a parent, I look quickly away.

I have pretended even to myself that Katie doesn't want to play hockey. I won't admit that I might say anything other than "yes!" to opportunities for my children.

But in the summer, at swim lessons, a lifeguard asked my Katie, "Do you play hockey just like your brother?"

My mom overheard Katie's answer, and it surprised me.

Katie said, "No. My mom says one hockey player in the family is enough. She won't let me play."

I won't let her play?

"I did not say that," I explained in horror when my mom told me.

Except that I did. Of course, I said it. One hockey player in the family *is* enough. I just didn't think Katie *heard* me say it.

143

And, I assure myself, if Katie really, really wanted to play — if she *loved* it — I would let her play. I would have to. I'm just really hoping she doesn't.

I'm avoiding exposing her to hockey is how I like to put it.

"Good strategery," Marty says. He pronounces it stra-tee-ja-ree, one of the many tics of a long relationship, an invented word that only we find funny.

Over the holidays, I wonder if our strategery should have also included working harder to avoid exposing Ollie to hockey. Life has a lot more give without hockey. We sleep late on weekends. We leave evenings free so we can go with the flow, do whatever comes up. We ski hard in the afternoons, not worried about wearing out leg muscles before practice. Ollie and his little buddies treat every outing to the hill like an epic adventure.

"Hold tight, Félix! We're coming to get you!"

"I'm in deep! But I've still got one ski." Félix bellows down slope to his friends.

"Ten-four! We're on our way. Rescue mission initiated."

Ollie and Sebastian climb up the mountain through hip-deep snow to save Félix. In reality, they're directly under the Bear Chair, and they climb about five yards, but in their imaginations they're deeply immersed in a backcountry survival situation. I reward their fortitude with hot chocolate and beaver tails.

Without hockey, we don't think ahead to meals. We avoid the mad race to get everyone fed by five p.m. If we eat late, we eat late. Who knew life with kids could be so easy?

Marty takes a week off during the holidays too and directs the extra energy toward his slow cooker. We eat quinoa black bean stew, lamb saag, downhome country shrimp, spicy pulled pork, Guinness beef ribs. It all cooks itself while I snuggle on the couch with my rosy-cheeked, strong-legged babies.

I am happy. Mostly. But when my mind drifts toward Thomas, I feel a heavy ache just below my breast bone. I cringe in embarrassment at my own greed. Look at all I have and still I'm not satisfied.

Husband good provider: check.
Husband loving father: check.
Husband good cook: check.
Kids healthy: check.
Kids happy: check.
Home comfortable: check.
I have everything.
But not quite everything.
The thing I want? The thing I imagine fulfilled by Thomas? It's not love. I have love.

But I want to look in a man's eyes and see fervent, new desire. I'm afraid that part of my life has drawn to a close. Even amid this family happiness, I hold his January visit in the back of my mind.

I try not to think beyond the visit. During the week of email exchanges, I felt a hint of the sadness that will follow our goodbye. But now that I've had space to let the emotion die down, I know it won't be him that I mourn. The grief has more to do with my own sexuality, rather than the man who temporarily reminded me of it. I want to be something not contained in my roles of hockey chauffer and skate sharpener. I want to hold on to the part of me that existed before hockey mom.

Until now I had kept very quiet about Thomas. I hadn't told a single person about this extracurricular flirtation. I liked the idea of him as a secret friend, visible only to me, sort of like Mr. Snuffleupagus except sexier. But his wife knowing about me has made him real. Suddenly I want to talk about him, about our connection. I want to make sense of why something so insignificant feels so big. To bridge this uncomfortable disconnect between my inner life and my outer one, I slip pieces of him into my day-to-day conversation, almost surprising myself to hear my inappropriate words hanging awkwardly in the air.

I kind of fell for this guy.
His wife found out about our flirtation.
Marty doesn't know. Not that there's anything to know. Not really.

Don't you sometimes feel it's impossible to get everything from one person, from one life partner?

What happens when a person changes after marriage? When a person wants different things in a mate?

I've never been good at small talk. I'm getting significantly worse.

I need to talk to an old friend from far away. On the phone to her, I hint at the nature of my pseudo-transgression. "Are you happy in marriage?" I can't help prying, holding everyone's relationship as a mirror to my own. "You feel like you could be happy with him forever?"

She's busy too, three boys in hockey, one of them traveling the province with an elite team. She and her husband both work too hard. They haven't had a trip alone together since the birth of their first child fourteen years ago. Marriage maintenance falls far down on their priority list. "Happy?" she says. "I don't know about that, but I put my kids first. I decided that when I became a mom. A marital collapse would be terribly disruptive for them."

I often look to this friend for guidance, but I'm skeptical of this martyr approach to parenting, to motherhood in particular. "But don't you think they'll be happier if you're happy, and that they can tell when a marriage is unsatisfying?"

"What am I going to do," she says. "Strike up an illicit relationship with some guy at a conference? I don't want to be a cliché."

That stings. "And staying in a marriage for the children? That's less of a cliché?"

Now we're both hurt and our conversation limps along. But neither of us wants to hang up angry. "You're smarter than I am," I finally say, conciliatory, "and better at doing the right thing. I always want the fun-in-the-moment thing. You've taken better care of your marriage too. But do you guys still kiss? Do you neck?"

I know I ask questions I shouldn't. I'm too open, too intimate. It's embarrassing. There's probably a name for this tendency but

I'm not sure I believe in modern day psychology on this front. What we're so fast to label disorder might simply be personality.

"No," my friend answers. She sounds conciliatory too, or maybe just tired. "We don't kiss. Kissing feels weird after all these years. Like there's too much baggage."

"I guess that's what I mean. I miss kissing. I'm not ready to say goodbye to that part of life."

Marty and I don't get back there over the break, back to kissing. We don't push through the rough patch onto a better and blissful other side. But we do relax into each other's company. We have a good break. A great break.

• • •

But on the last night of holidays, as Marty makes his lunch for work and we gear up to return to the schedule shuffle, I feel the energy shifting. Already we're bracing against the constant compromise, the ever-growing resentment.

"Ollie has a hockey tournament right away in the new year," I say. "In Kimberley. I've got a work event, in Lethbridge, so you'll have to take him. And a colleague . . . a friend . . . is coming from the States. He's never been to the Canadian Rockies so before our event I'm going to take a few days to show him around — maybe a backcountry lodge, maybe a hike-in hot springs, that kind of thing — and then he flies out of Cranbrook on Saturday morning. I'll come relieve you from the tournament and you can get back in time to pick Katie up from ski racing."

Marty glazes over. I've given him too much information. He stopped listening sometime around the word "colleague." His mental hard drive has reached maximum capacity. I know that. I'm taking advantage and using my control over the family calendar in a way I never have before. I would not like to describe myself as manipulative, but in this moment no other word fits. Marty doesn't even ask about my friend.

"So I'm going where?" His voice comes out gruff, thick with fatigue at the mere thought of returning to work and hockey and schedules. "Where and when? Give me the need-to-know."

"On Friday night, you're taking Ollie to Kimberley for a game, staying the night at St. Eugene Resort, and then taking him back to Kimberley for another game early Saturday morning. I'll be there to tag-team you before second period. You can still ski Saturday afternoon." Oh, my generosity! *You don't worry about Saturday, honey — you go ski!* I have shaped this story with remarkable agility and ease.

"Okay," he says, simply.

"Okay. Also Ollie's skates need to be sharpened."

"Okay." Marty wants me to stop talking. He's making his lunch. Marty does one thing at a time and he does it perfectly. My talk of schedules interrupts him in a way he finds irritating. So easily we slide into our post-holiday roles.

"Okay," I hesitate. I have just used hockey to get myself a couple days alone with a man who my husband doesn't know. A man whose wife disapproves of the nature of our correspondence. This should not be so easy. "Okay," I say again, making my voice light, cheerful. "Thanks. Perfect." I don't know what exactly I think I'm doing, but "*Perfect*"? I nearly choke on the word. I have become something I never thought I would be. I am a liar, liar pants on fire.

CHAPTER EIGHT

BAD HOCKEY MOM

On the evening I drive to the Cranbrook airport to pick up Thomas, I feel like a teenage girl preparing for her first date. I don't want to be too early. I don't want to be too late. I select my clothes carefully. I don't want to look like I tried too hard. But I don't want to look like I didn't try at all. I know it's wrong — my excitement to see him. Even as I push through the airport doors, I half doubt he'll be there. When my mind has drifted his way over the last three weeks, I've fluctuated between a conviction he'll never show up and a desire that when he does show up, he'll dismiss the melodrama concerning his wife as his idea of a practical joke.

Then there he is in Cranbrook, B.C., walking toward me in the serious winter coat and the heavy-duty winter boots that I advised him to wear when I warned him about our unusually cold year.

"You're here," I say. "Surreal." He feels imaginary.

Before we get to the work part of the visit, we need to talk. I want to hear what happened, what's happening, in his own sentences, not his wife's.

"I don't want to spend your whole visit having serious emotional talks," I tell him in the dark car. "Partly because I'm guessing this will be the last time we'll see each other and I don't want to waste it, and partly because I suspect you've had enough serious, emotional conversations over the last month."

"Yes," he sighs, gratefully.

I start with the obvious question: *What happened?*

He'd been distracted, he tells me, and his wife suspected he'd directed his attention elsewhere. "She's a bit psychic," he says. "She pays close attention to my schedule." Piecing together where he'd been and who he talked about, and who he stopped talking about, she pulled my name out of thin air one day. "I put up a feeble resistance at first," he says. "But I couldn't sustain it. I confessed."

His thoughts *had* been on me, then.

I see fatigue in his posture. He folds in on himself. When I've pictured him over the past few months, I've imagined his shoulders back, his chest out. I remembered the intensity of his eyes. But today, he crosses his arms over his chest and hunches his shoulders. He stares at the dashboard, not at me. Nearly fifteen years older than Marty, Thomas is still handsome, in a way that has more to do with his intellectual energy than his physical appearance. As he speaks, I study him, wondering what about this Thomas has so drawn my attention away from my own husband. He's not better than Marty, at all, but he's different.

"Our little flirtation is over," I say. "I know that. I get it. The whole obsessiveness of it . . ." I wave my hand around, I don't need to say what he knows. "Unhealthy. Distracting. We both need to get back to our real lives. But I'm glad I met you and got to know you a bit." He nods. He's not saying much. I've wondered before if his silence is a strategy. His attentive listening and his private nature leave him a blank slate onto which women can project their fantasies. He can be whatever I want him to be.

Today, I must be nervous. I can't stop myself from chattering to fill the space. "*Why you?* That's what I wonder. I meet lots of talented men, funny men, smart men, handsome men. It's not like you're the only smart, handsome man I've ever met. But I don't react like this. Not typically. Thank goodness."

"The me you're drawn to," he says into the windshield, "is a fantasy. In real life you'd find me annoying. I'd bore you. I watch a lot of bad TV."

"It's about male affirmation," I say. Of course I *know* he's only a fantasy, but telling him so seems rude. I change the subject. "That's my pattern. Because I didn't get male affirmation growing up. As an adult, every time I get in a new group, I find the best man and I try to make him fall in love with me. To prove myself worthy of male attention. When my brother wrestled, I married the most handsome wrestler in the country. When I swam, I married the guy on my team with the most beautiful butterfly. Now I'm in the academic community. I set my sights on you."

"See," he says, meeting my eyes for a fraction of a second. I spot generosity. "That's wisdom."

"Hm." I don't want to be wise.

"These things never end well." His voice stays quiet. His brief sentences feel rehearsed. He's been sent to me with a script.

I can't think of anything to say into this changing friendship. We listen to the tires against the pavement until he asks, "How old are your kids?"

My kids. I feel the phrase as a clunk in my gut. He and I have never talked about real life. We've known each other nearly two years, and this is the first time he's asked anything about my children. I didn't even know his wife's name until I started getting the plural-pronoun emails. But now he asks, *How old are your kids?* The question signals the end of our make-believe.

"Just turned ten and nearly eight."

"They're young."

"Yep, they're young." There's really not much to say after that. I am a mother with young children. This flirtation has no place in my life.

He doesn't ask how I've orchestrated these days away from Ollie and Katie and Marty. We say nothing until the silence becomes uncomfortable. I'm the first to break it. "I knew this thing would have to come to an end. I've told myself our little emails don't hurt anyone. But I've lied. I know we're both distracted. That hurts your people and my people. It hurts us too."

"Yes. And now I'm here so we can find a way to settle into a simple friendship?" I think I hear a gentle mocking behind his rehearsed words.

"We're *not* going to be simple friends," I say.

"No, probably not."

"But I am going to introduce you to everyone that way. *This is Thomas, my simple friend.*"

The laughter helps us relax into each other's company so we can enjoy our goodbye visit. He's been flattered by my attention, he says. He has true affection for me. He's appreciated my kindness and generosity. As he speaks, I feel myself calming down. I've been revved up on this guy. Given the choice, I like to run high. But it's not sustainable. I have a life and he's not part of it. I have people counting on me.

"There," I tell him, as we merge onto the main highway. "I'm good now. We'll have a fun few days, and then we'll go back to our real lives."

• • •

152

In our days together, I wonder if I'm proving my Massachusetts psychologist friend wrong. Maybe I *can* have all the lives. These hours running childless around the Rocky Mountains with my brilliant, brown-eyed friend certainly exist separate from the life of "Angie, the hockey mom" or "Angie, the miner's wife." I immerse myself in these days. I will take the happiness they bring. Then I can go back to my other life, real life. I'll bring this new energy with me. Charged up, I will be a better mother, a better wife. This break will be good for everyone. I say it to myself until I believe it. *Welcome to the Rockies,* I want to say on Thomas's second day. It takes a few hours of hot-springing, but then he's here with me. He unfurls quickly. He forgets he's not supposed to look at me. He returns to speaking in his own sentences. There's no more talk of our simple friendship.

Research indicates athletes tend to become attached to over-stimulation and have trouble with regular life. I once thought swimmers partied hard because their senses were deprived in all those underwater hours, making them want to live more intensely when they came up for air. But driving through the Tim Hortons one day, a CBC Radio program about swimming caught my attention. I texted Marty: Turn on radio. Swimming! X

The CBC broadcaster explained that when swimmers move fast through the water, every part of their skin is stimulated. Plus the dopamine and serotonin and endorphins coursing through their bodies in response to the hard physical work create a natural high. Athletes become addicted to these highs and struggle to adjust to post-competitive life. Alcohol abuse is prevalent among athletes. I wonder if marital breakdowns are as well.

• • •

On Thomas's last day in Canada, we visit a backcountry lodge, accessible only by snow cat. As the treaded machine carries us up the steep slope, through the old-growth cedar forest, and above the clouds, Thomas asks me about my past in sports.

"Did you like coaching swimming?"

"I loved it." I realize my love only as I declare it. "I loved teaching swimming far more than I like teaching writing."

He's surprised and asks me to elaborate.

"Because you *can* actually teach someone how to swim. You tell them what to do and they do it. They practice until they get it. Then you tell them the next thing. And they get that too. And then *they can swim!*"

We laugh, recognizing the utility of this skill in comparison to the writing skills we teach.

He extrapolates my swimming analogy into an imagined writing workshop: "You're still drowning, but you're drowning more slowly now. Or you're still drowning but this time you didn't take us all down with you."

It's lovely — crawling through the old-growth forest, laughing with a man who shares my passions, who understands what I do for a living. A man with whom I will never have a single conversation about credit card bills or school report cards or household chores or hockey camp.

• • •

At the airport, our goodbye is quick.

"So we probably won't stay in touch," Thomas says. "I won't send the usual thank-you message for organizing and hosting. I'll say it now. Thank you."

"You're welcome," I say. I know this is how things have to be: goodbye, thank you, you're welcome, goodbye. I can be tough about it, I think.

"You'll be okay?"

Why does everyone keep asking me that? Has he been taking instructions from Ollie?

"I will be okay," I say. "I just need to change my approach. I thought we could let this little attraction run its course, and if we just spent enough time together we'd get sick of each other." I smile. "That's not working."

"No," he agrees, shuffling his feet like a shy teenager, but his smile is not shy. His smile is trouble.

"So instead, I'll be grateful for the time we had. It's been good. We both need to redirect our attention to our own lives, our own people."

We hug quickly, and I'm gone, on my way to the Kimberley arena. I don't cry over this friendship's conclusion, and I won't for two weeks.

I have the thirty-minute drive from the airport to get myself rink-ready. The illusion of me being the sole hockey parent has disintegrated. With the distraction of Thomas gone, I become aware of the burn in my eyes, the hint of nausea. How much did I sleep last night? And how much did I drink?

I expect Marty to look at the bags under my bloodshot eyes and greet me with a snarky "Quality parenting, Ang!" Instead, he smiles my way and all the other parents throw their arms in the air to celebrate my mid-game arrival: "Angie! You're here!" Sharon, Melissa, Amanda, Vivian — this far into the season they've become a family of sorts.

"I'm here!" I mirror their enthusiasm, flinging my arms above my head.

"Wow," Marty says, pushing down the bench to give me his warmed spot. "You're popular. Nobody does that when I show up. You're like Norm from *Cheers*. The hockey arena: the place where everyone knows your name."

I expect that once my arrival excuses Marty from hockey duties, he will race off to the ski hill, to get in a few fast runs before he has to find Katie, but instead he puts his arm around me and pulls me close to his side. Together, we watch our son play. As hard as marriage is, and as easy as it is to fantasize about

the intellectual and artistic life I might have with one of the brilliant men I meet on the conference circuit, *nobody* else would do
this with me. No other man in the world would sit with me and
proudly watch my B-team, third-line player. Nobody else would
love Ollie like I do. If Marty had caught me in my conniving, in
my deliberate and self-serving manipulation of the schedule, even
if he had publicly scolded me for my hangover, I could not feel
worse than I do now, with his arm wrapped tightly around me.
Nothing could make me feel as bad this morning as his kindness
and his love do. His shared enthusiasm for Ollie's sport drowns
me in guilt.

"Thanks," I say, putting my hand on his knee and slowly running it up and down his quad. The fastest kicker on our varsity
swim team, he still has strong legs. In recent years, he has complained that I never touch him anymore. He looks at me surprised now, his face softening, reminding me of the way we used
to look at each other, fifteen years ago.

"Thanks for what?" He's handsome when he smiles. He shares
Ollie's implausible moss-green eyes.

"For doing everything," I say. "For all you do. I appreciate it."

He's confused by my rare articulation of gratitude. But he'll
take it. He slides his hand down my waist and scooches me his
way until our hips touch. He kisses my cheek.

"Fnanks," I say. It's the way Ollie said thank you at two. We
still copy him, when we're feeling sentimental or vulnerable or
scared. *Fnanks.*

"You know I'll do whatever you ask. No problem, Ang."

Right. No problem. We're all good. I dig in my handbag for
an ibuprofen. I really do have a headache.

CHAPTER NINE

MORE BAD
HOCKEY MOMS

Marty leaves the Kimberley rink, and I submerge myself in spectating. I Am Hockey Mom. I won't think outside of that. I push Thomas out of my mind, but I do let myself feel him as a pleasant buzz. I'll ride that hormonal upswing for weeks. I wonder how long the high will eclipse the less pleasant remnants of the visit. This up will come with a crash.

The kids are awful. They didn't practice once over Christmas holidays, and now they return to the rink straight into a tournament. Maybe my emotionally raw state has made me irritable, but this quick move to competition irks me. There should not be a game after two weeks with no practice. I feel the same way about the track meets at my kids' school: the children show up for a competition without ever having been taught how to shotput, high jump, or long jump, without ever training for the running races at all.

Competitions without practice miss the point of sport. The value in athletics comes in learning to dedicate oneself to repetitive work, struggling to perfect a skill, training hard in hopes of shining at competition. Without those stages of preparation, the competition means nothing.

The kids know this at some level. They haven't invested any energy in preparing, so they don't care whether they win or lose. In the first game I watch, they lose five to three. Nobody cries. None of the kids express any emotion at all. The parents seem relieved. "Oh good, we won't be in the final tomorrow. We can get home before dark."

In terms of effort, the weekend is a mixed bag. Sometimes the kids show up. Sometimes they don't. Either way, the parents sit in the cold stands: watching, watching, watching. The lethargic play bores me.

But every now and then, Ollie strides onto the ice a streak of pure energy. He "plays like his head is on fire," we say. "Sometimes he plays like he's *crazy*," the coach has said, reminding me of Roland's comment that you have to be a bit nuts to be an athlete. "Crazy Ollie" flies. Wherever the puck goes, he's there. He wants it. He's a blur. Hilarious to watch, he barely controls his own energy. He could explode at any second, head over heels, equipment flying. I can't help smiling, but I watch through my fingers.

But again Roland sees something I don't. "You have an athlete on your hands," he says, calmly, his arms crossed over his chest, a smile toying at the corners of his mouth. Roland makes the pronouncement with such confidence that I don't think to contradict him. "Just look at him go." Something about Ollie's performance pleases Roland. As much as Roland has been dismissive — even condemnatory — of that nutty athlete mindset, I wonder if he misses it, a little.

His assessment of Ollie reminds me again of the difference

between athlete *selection* and *identification*. A coach picking a team to win right now would not select Ollie, but clearly Roland identifies something in Ollie that portends future ability, though maybe not necessarily in hockey. My brother sees it too. "One day Ollie will be great at something, whatever it is," Justin says. The thing these two Olympians admire? Ollie's intensity.

Partway through the second game, my fear comes true. Ollie fails to rein in his own speed and exuberance. He slides into the boards so hard I feel the crash in my own rib cage. All the parents' heads swivel to me. I'm out of my seat ready to race down to the ice, but before I get past the knees and the popcorn, Ollie pops back up.

"Tough kid," Roland says with the same amused smile.

"Pain is just like comfort," Ollie tells me after the game. "Well, not like comfort. But pain's just another feeling."

Oh dear. Maybe Roland is right. Maybe I do have an athlete on my hands.

I wonder if Ollie can do the same with his emotions. "Can you try that with your anger? With sadness? Maybe you can think of those kinds of feelings as just another feeling?"

I'm forever attempting to mine sport for life lessons, to make sense of all the time and money we spend at the rink. Ollie struggled at the start of this school year. The move away from his school's sport program, Hockey Academy, has been successful, and Ollie no longer associates the sport with stress. Hockey has transformed into pure fun. But the anxiety-related behaviors he'd been demonstrating at the rink still bubbled up at school, during the early months of grade four. He cried easily. When he struggled with the work, his stress escalated quickly too, making the work even more challenging. At his worst, he engaged in self-harm. I take solace in the fact that he has never turned his frustration outward, has never hit another child or a teacher. But he has hit himself.

I suspect the self-harm at school is caused by the same

frustrations that provoked the incident at Hockey Academy the time he skated headfirst hard into the boards: helplessness in the face of too much pressure, too little flexibility, too much stress, and not enough valuing of him as he is. I'd like him to change schools, and I've pitched the idea of putting him in the lower-pressure public school, which has more resources to help him with stress management. But neither Marty nor Ollie likes change. So far, I've been losing the switch-school fight, and, in the classroom, Ollie sometimes loses the fight against his own anxiety.

"Maybe hockey can teach you that, Ollie — how to control your emotions the way you control your response to physical pain."

• • •

As the weekend wears on, I realize the team's lackluster perfor-mance has roots beyond the lack of practice over the holiday season. Here, as we approach the last six weeks of the season, we find a new kind of Atom team on the ice. In December, the Fernie Canadian Tire sponsored a program called First Shift. Like the American JumpStart program, First Shift allows kids from underprivileged families to try hockey. Canadian Tire provides the equipment, and the kids (ages six to ten) get six weeks of lessons, all at no cost. At the end of the program, the nine- and ten-year-old children have the opportunity to join the Atom team midseason. On our team, three newbies join. The program included three other teams in the Kootenays, none in our league.

I should be in favor of this program. I *am* in favor of this pro-gram. In theory. First Shift responds to one of my main criticisms of hockey: that it's become a cheque-book sport, available only to the well-off. In a 2013 *Globe and Mail* article, James Mirtle writes, "It's widely known that Canada's national winter sport is expensive to play. But various factors have conspired over the last ten to fifteen years to make minor hockey dramatically more expensive, pricing out many middle-class families, let alone lower-class ones and new Canadians. These days, more and more of the players who go on to play major junior, college, and, ultimately, pro hockey are from wealthy backgrounds." Kids whose parents can afford $20,000 a year for sport schools will beat the blue-collar kids who once shared an opportunity to make it to the big league. In *Selling the Dream: How Hockey Parents and Their Kids Are Paying the Price for Our National Obsession,* Jim Parcels, a long-time minor hockey coach and administrator, writes, "If you're doing eight, nine, ten years of Triple A hockey from novice up, you're talking eight to ten grand, minimum." In a 2014 *Edmonton Sun* article, Mary-Kay Messier, director of brand initiatives with Bauer and sister to Edmonton Oilers legend Mark Messier, said research shows that nine out of ten kids in Canada are not playing hockey; ninety percent of Canadian children miss out on the benefits of the sport and participating in the culture of hockey so synonymous with Canadian childhood. In over thirty cities and towns across Canada, First Shift began in order to address this inequity. Messier lent his support to the program, claiming that since hockey is such a part of the Canadian identity, we should do our best to offer the experience to all kids, even ones whose parents cannot afford thousands of dollars per year.

I support that fully. Absolutely. In theory.

But suddenly, in this January game, we have children on the ice who do not understand offside, who cannot skate well, and who never touch the puck. Essentially, the team plays short-handed every shift while a wayward new player holds him or herself up with a hockey stick at the wrong end of the rink. We more competitive parents console ourselves: at least down there, the new player won't get in the way! Even at this relatively non-competitive level, the parents have begun to grumble. In fact, a few strangely competitive and hostile behaviors manifest throughout the weekend.

Here's another downside of children specializing in sport too young: I can clearly see on the ice before me that kids who don't start at five years old have a hard time catching up. We already know that kids with late-in-the-year birthdays struggle in hockey — and since they don't shine, they get less coaching attention and less ice time than the more physically mature kids. Every year, the gap widens. If kids born in December can't keep up, how will kids three or four years behind catch up? To give children a true opportunity at a late start in this game, hockey culture would require a major shift in ideology and a long-term plan to fully accommodate and incorporate those new players. Giving them a one-time injection of cash won't dissolve the true barriers.

Simply put, North American kids get good at hockey too early and winning matters too much, to the coaches and to the parents, at least.

One parent seeking assurance that her son would be okay to join hockey after ten years of age started a forum thread asking for examples of successful players who did not begin playing young. The best hockey fans could offer? Ovechkin, who started at age eight. Eight is an example of an old start?

• • •

In a 2015 *Washington Post* article, Petula Dvorak writes, "Our ten-year-old decided to give ice hockey a try. What we encountered was dreadful." She explains that her son demonstrated early talent at skating but had no interest in hockey until he hit the double digits. Her conclusion? "Turns out, he was waaaaay over the hill. At ten." She explains that at age ten kids were already doing six o'clock morning practices, goalie clinics, off-ice conditioning, travel tournaments, and personal-trainer sessions. I can see how this level of commitment seems outrageous to a hockey-parenting newbie. It's my normal. It's normal for every hockey parent in North America. But I hear Dvorak loud and clear when she expresses astonishment at "the madness that has become youth sports in this country." Her ten-year-old son had to play with the four- and five-year-olds. Worse yet, he found himself out-skated by them all. As I sit in Kimberley watching these new-comer ten-year-olds try to blend in with kids their own age, I see the wisdom of starting them out with younger kids, despite the inherent humiliation.

"Whoooooops," I mutter, as the referee stops another of our players, mid-breakaway. Skater offside, again. Our team can't even make it down to the other net, let alone take a shot. "There's gotta be another way to get the new kids out there. Let them do a half season with Novice first. Find their feet."

"Yes." The kindest mom on our team nods her head. This last offside halted her son's breakaway. "That's what my husband and I think too. For their own safety. It's dangerous for them to be out there. They can barely skate."

"Yes. Exactly. For their safety."

We hide our frustration and vicarious competitiveness behind a half-baked concern for the new kids' well-being.

"Oh no!" I lift my hands to my face as a First Shift player falls over and accidently pushes the puck into her own net. "Damn."

God, Angie, really? This player's mom could be sitting right behind me.

"Sorry," I say to myself. "It's fine. It's just a game. They're learning."

Sometimes I am the kind of hockey parent I hate.

The Hockey Canada website pinpoints ages five to eight as key in development of hockey skating. American hockey programs suggest the same starting age. Minnesota Hockey, for example, is standard in recommending that kids don't start hockey before age five, though they can work on their skating from two to four. The Minnesota site counters these alarmingly young starting ages with an encouraging: "It is never too late to start playing hockey. Players have joined hockey programs at twelve to thirteen years old and still made varsity hockey teams. More importantly, the expansion of college intramural and adult teams have made hockey a lifetime sport."

A sweet sentiment, but I don't believe it. Their theory does not match the reality before my eyes. To give these kids a real chance, they will need extra coaching and extra ice-time. When they graduate to Pee Wee in a year, they will get less of each. In Pee Wee, coaches no longer have an official obligation to play the kids evenly. Playing to win, coaches bench the weak players and focus on the best. First Shift is a Band-Aid applied to a deep, infected wound.

This ineffectiveness holds true on the class issue as well as the late-start issue. First Start pays for equipment for one season, but if the children decide to continue, who will cover the cost of fees and equipment and travel the next season? And the season after that? First Shift gives these kids a taste of the sport: *here is something you can't have.*

On his worst days, Ollie cannot keep up at this level and he started skating at three. He joined his first hockey team at five. How would a novice twelve-year-old have a chance with these kids two more years down the road? The sport does not have a functioning late-integration strategy.

By the time Ollie hits Pee Wee next year, all the First Shift kids will have disappeared. In fact, all the players the same level or weaker than Ollie will have dropped out of hockey in favor of other sports — sports that offer a recreational, fun option; sports that require less of a parental commitment; sports that are more affordable.

• • •

In the car to the hotel, Ollie grumbles about the game. He's irritable and doesn't know why. I have my theories. They have to do with effort in (little), reward out (little), but I keep those thoughts to myself. I'm tired and hungover and a little sad. I leave Ollie to pick at the scab of his own irritation.

164

"That guy tripped me. The ref didn't even call it. I could have scored. If *I* tried tripping someone, the ref would see *that*!"

I don't meet his eyes or offer any sympathy. "You could try swimming instead. Nobody trips in swimming. Ever."

I can hear him humphing and fidgeting, but I still don't look for him in the rearview mirror. "Just because Grandma and Grandpa love golf doesn't mean they make you play golf."

"When I was little, Grandma loved swimming. Grandpa loved wrestling."

I can't resist a glance to the mirror to see him puzzling through the family history. Grandma loved swimming. I swam. Grandpa loved wrestling. Uncle Justin wrestled.

"Oh. Well."

Katie would have come back with a sassy *Well, Grandma and Grandpa don't make you golf now!* Ollie broods.

He comes to life at the hotel, though. Both the kids and the parents seem more interested in the hotel pool than the hockey rink. We've splurged on a resort for this tournament and we all race through dinner to meet at the outdoor recreation area: two hot tubs and a pool warm enough to swim even though it's January. The kids go wild. The hotel likely has a no-alcohol-on-deck rule but nobody follows it. A team of moms huddles on the pool edge, three bottles of wine at their feet. I think I recognize them as the parents from Golden, but they keep saying — loudly — "We're from *Lillooet*!" Lillooet has no team in the tournament, and I'm not sure whether they intend their Lillooet cover to protect them from their kids' behavior or their own behavior. *Hockey Moms Gone Wild!*

"Hey!" I greet them with a complicit smile. "I'm from Lillooet too!"

Before I had kids, I thought this kind of social life a little pathetic. My childhood friends who had their kids younger told me: we don't really have friends anymore — we have other hockey parents. The late-night drinking in hotel hallways struck me as a poor stand-in for real friendship, a poor stand-in for a real life. Now as a working mother, I'm grateful for a couple glasses of wine with some fun moms. Marty and I rarely make time to socialize. Without the hockey-parent hotel parties, I'd have little female companionship in my life at all. The tie to alcohol worries me, though. A hockey mom from Whitefish told me a parent on her team makes apple pie moonshine and they drink it at the six a.m. weekend practices, calling it "Pies and Shine!" The ease with which she confessed these morning drinks shocked me, even coming as it did over a shared bottle of wine, but we "Lillooet Moms" are no better. Early last season, my gang took turns bringing wine to Friday night practices. We'd sit in the stands with our coffee mugs, red staining our teeth. We did that for a few weeks, quite pleased with the way we'd spiced up our schedule, until a dad turned his stare on us and said, "Is that booze in those mugs?" The judgment in his voice killed our enthusiasm for the Friday night ritual. We're not alone, though — hockey moms and wine, it's a thing. The *National Post* ran a story on a group of moms who rent a limo to go to their Atom games so they can drink in the stands without worrying about the drive back to the hotel.

It's the boredom that makes alcohol so tempting. We parents have relegated ourselves to the sidelines of our kids' lives. They act. We watch. Alcohol helps us blur the tedium of that existence. It lets us pretend we're not only spectating as our kids have fun, but we're having our own fun too.

Medical professionals mark high-risk drinking lower than we might think. A man who has five drinks one day a week falls into high-risk territory. Four drinks one evening per week puts a woman in that same alcohol-abuse zone. Moderate drinking comes with health benefits: we can enjoy a drink or even two per evening without guilt or concern. But moderation rarely features in athletic culture. I've started to measure and count my drinks and keep an eye on alcohol content because I know if I lie to myself about how much I drink, I lie to myself about who I am.

I've not yet got my weekly count as low as I would like.

This weekend, though, I'm buzzing from the high of Thomas's visit — and let's be honest I'm still a little hungover — so I don't feel alcohol's pull. I easily pass on this party, but I do get a kick out of the Golden moms from Lillooet. They huddle in parkas and under blankets, backs turned to the pool, absorbed in their own laughter. They look like old friends. They look happy. They could be a commercial for merlot. Or for Canada.

In the pool, their boys have struck up a war against our boys (the girls knew enough to leave). The Fernie group hides behind a fortress of patio tables and chairs, hurling snowballs at the Golden kids. It strikes me that they believe their on-ice rivalry. Quickly the Golden team constructs its own fort on the opposite side of the pool. Bombs fly. In the hot tub, we Fernie parents try to take a cue from the Golden moms and ignore the scene too.

"That's just snow they're throwing, right?" Amanda can't quite repress her parental concern. As a nurse, she can imagine all the ways this mini-war could go wrong. "Quinn! Quit running. You guys. *Walk.*" She lifts her beer bottle to me in a toast. "There. Did my part."

"Owww. Jeez. That's ice."

I look up to see Quinn grabbing his head with a hostile stare at the enemy fort. I flip into lifeguard mode, marching to the side of the pool, hands on hips. I wish for a whistle. "OKAY! NOW! KIDS FROM FERNIE ON THAT SIDE. KIDS FROM GOLDEN ON THAT SIDE. DO NOT GO NEAR EACH OTHER. OR EVERYONE GOES HOME. NOW. I MEAN IT."

Wet shirtless boys from both sides look at me with wide-eyed obedience, steam rising from their bodies, all shocked to stillness, until a little goggle-eyed kid pops up. He stays above the water just long enough to announce: "We're not from Golden! We're from *Lillooet!*"

The declaration dissolves his Golden teammates into guffaws, breaking my spell of authority.

We let the snowball war go for another ten minutes and then drag the kids off to bed.

On the way to the room, Ollie slides his hand into mine and asks me questions about the Indigenous portraits and art on the walls. I tell him that St. Eugene Mission Resort used to be a residential school. "The Ktunaxa got their land back, and they decided to make something out of it. I would have burned the whole place to the ground. But they want the residential school building to stand as a reminder to everyone of what white people did to their people. The casino, the golf course — that's their way of answering to history."

"What's a residential school?" Ollie loves history, and I know once he grabs on to this story, I will have to study up. He will want dates and numbers. He'll remember them all.

"The white government took Ktunaxa kids away from their own parents and put them in boarding schools, in this very building. The teachers, priests, and nuns sometimes beat the children. Parents missed their kids. A whole generation grew up without their language. It led to . . . well, a lot of bad things for the Ktunaxa people. This resort is their way of rebuilding."

Ollie feels every word of this story, even censored as it is. "They took kids away from their parents? Why would grown-ups do that?!"

I will never be able to answer all of his questions. "I don't know, Ollie." He has a way of highlighting how little I understand about the world.

The St. Eugene resort is pure luxury, but I'm also uneasy within its walls. It feels haunted. Also, I can't reconcile the natural splendor — the Fisher Peak, the hoodoos, the Rocky Mountains, the Kootenay forest, the St. Mary's River — with the historical horrors that happened here. I look up and wonder how the priests and nuns could look at this beauty every morning and then do what they did. It's naïve, I know.

Ollie keeps talking while we get ready for bed and while we snuggle in together, pulling the warm blankets up to our chins.

"How many Ktunaxa people are there in the world?"

"Where do they live?"

"What does their language sound like?"

"Do they have a religion?"

"Do you have any Ktunaxa friends?"

"Do they know their parents?"

"Did bad things happen to them?"

"Did they play hockey?"

His persistent questions uncover a heavy story, one I'm reluctant to share with him, but still I'm grateful for this evening together. It reminds me of my favorite part of hockey: conversations alone with my boy. I could talk to him for hours, about whatever he wants.

Tonight we talk about the racism of residential schools and the racism of hockey. I don't tell him that according to a 2017 article in the *Toronto Star* there were fewer than thirty Black players in the NHL in 2016, making hockey the whitest of sports. In the essay, sport columnist Bruce Arthur talks about the strain of racism lurking in hockey and tells stories of fans throwing banana peels at black players or shouting that they should go back to basketball where they belong. I also don't tell Ollie that in a 2015 essay called "Why the Ice Is White," Wes Judd attempts to explain why the NHL remains the most segregated professional sport league. He cites extensive research pointing the finger at cost. Those families with more disposable income gravitate toward this expensive sport, and the United States continues to have "a stark race-to-wealth differential." In other words, wealthier means whiter. Because the fan base traditionally mirrors the lack of diversity modeled on the ice, non-white youth lack exposure to hockey, and their exclusion from the sport becomes a "self-perpetuating loop." Bruce Arthur quotes William Douglas, the author of a blog called *The Color of Hockey*, to explain the cyclical nature of this white, affluent feedback loop. Douglas claims, "Not seeing players of color on the ice on a regular basis or not knowing there are players of color . . . reinforces the stereotype. Then it becomes a self-fulfilling prophecy."

I don't tell Ollie any of that, but I wonder if the same prophecy has played out with Indigenous athletes.

"I don't know much about Ktunaxa people and hockey," I tell him. "But I know the first Indigenous player in the NHL was Fred Sasakamoose. In 1953." Ollie likes dates. "He played for the Canucks in my hometown before he made the NHL."

"Sasakamoose playing in Moose Jaw, Saskatchewan?" Ollie also likes sounds. He drags out the ooose on both names.

NativeHockey.com, a site that keeps track of Indigenous hockey past and present, lists only eight Indigenous players currently in the NHL. Ollie's Atom team is one hundred percent white.

In a 2017 *Hockey News* article, Janice Forsyth, director for the International Centre for Olympic Studies at Western University, discusses the scarcity of Indigenous players in the NHL. She identifies the same factors as Bruce Arthur did in his argument about players of color: financial challenges and lack of visibility on the world stage. Forsyth adds another challenge faced by remote, rural players: scouts simply don't see them. Urban kids have the advantage there, which works as another obstacle for many Indigenous communities.

"Carey Price is Indigenous," I say. Ollie's first ever hockey shirt, bought by his Habs-obsessed father, bore Price's name and number. Ollie is a Price fan, by birth. I wonder if Price will serve as a model for Indigenous youth the way players like Laraque and the Subbans have for Black players or Jujhar Khaira has for Indo-Canadians — and if hockey will gradually open up to a range of cultures and ethnicities and become more representative of North America in its entirety.

"Carey Price is Indigenous?"

"Yep."

Ollie stumbles over the word Indigenous, though I'm sure he's learned it at school. My Ktunaxa friend Anna Sam Hudson says she can tell when a person first learned about her culture by whether that person uses the term "Indian," "First Nations," "Aboriginal," or "Indigenous." I'm glad my son knows nothing of the "Indian" era.

At the Vancouver Writers Festival, I heard Cree comedian and novelist Dawn Dumont talk about her experience of racism. "I grew up in Saskatchewan," she said, "and I thought it was really racist. Then I left and I realized . . . *it was!* I had to leave the province to realize I am a person and I deserve to be treated like a person."

"You know why it matters, Ollie?"

"Why what matters?"

"Why there shouldn't just be white boys playing hockey? It's because we say hockey is Canada's game, but if only white Canadians are playing, it's not really Canada's game at all, is it?" I realize I have a new reason to be reluctant about my son's participation in hockey — its exclusiveness. "For hockey to be Canada's game, all Canadians need to get the same chance to play. But we don't see that. Where are the Indigenous players or the girl players or the players of color?"

"Yeah," Ollie agrees. "There's hardly any. That's kinda stupid."

Yes, Ollie, it's kinda stupid.

• • •

We stay up late talking, and the next day Ollie's performance remains mostly flat. The same is true for nearly all of his teammates. Except Jacob. Jacob shows up for the Sunday morning game, putting on a demo of dexterity, easily skating around the other team (and, to be honest, his own team) to score four goals.

His mom, Vivian, takes credit for this energy surge, boasting that she scolded him.

"*I'm not coming all this way to watch you play like shit!* That's what I told him. I pay a fortune for this sport. I've got a life." Vivian wears her white blonde hair in a boyish cut. I stare at her eye makeup, marveling at the detailed work. It looks professional. The most glamorous mom at the rink, she turns heads even when she's not putting on a show. "I don't need to be here. I'm here for him. But he's gotta do something too. Otherwise forget it."

I cringe at this strategy — the scolding and the threatening and the guilt — but I also wonder if I'm not doing enough, if I'm failing in my role as sport parent. Vivian's right: we do pay a lot and most of the kids have not been trying hard at all. Should I discipline Ollie when he doesn't try? Should I make sure he knows that this game costs us, not just financially? Should I insist on an effort in return for the cost? Will Ollie even learn how to put in a real solid effort if I don't require it of him? Is that my job? To teach him?

I weaken momentarily. Maybe Vivian is on to something, and we should hold our kids to account for playing badly, for not trying. They're not babies anymore, I guess.

Fernie Ghostriders lose that morning game and end up playing for last.

"We demand a recount," Amanda jokes.

"Zero plus zero makes zero no matter how you add it up," the coach says.

"Oh, well," we say, consoling ourselves, "at least they'll finally have an even game, a showdown between two teams that can't pull out a single victory."

And then in the game for last place, they somehow look even worse, lethargic and uninterested in the play going on around them. They work harder when they play against teams better than they are. Now in this even match, they don't try at all. They might as well be at home on their Xboxes. We could all be skiing. Even Jacob's scolding-induced skill-surge does not stick. Vivian leans forward in her seat and makes threating gestures at him. "Jacob, work! Skate!" But she's not the only one frustrated. All the parental yelling takes on an aggravated, mean tone.

"What are you guys doing out there?!"

"Move it!"

"Wake up!"

"Fuck."

We're sitting close to the Cranbrook parents, and they can hear all of this poor behavior. I'm embarrassed, but I can't help wondering: what *are* the kids doing out there?

Instead of watching the game, I text friends. I scroll through Facebook. I plan what I'll do when the tournament mercifully ends. I imagine myself reunited with the half-read copy of *All the Pretty Horses* waiting for me on my nightstand.

I don't want to watch one more second. But then, for no clear reason, our kids wake up going into the third period. Jonathan, the big defenseman, scores two goals from the blue line. Inspired, the coach moves Jonathan to offense, where he scores twice more. His goals seem to remind the other kids of the game's objective. They all charge for victory as we count down the game's final seconds. A 7–3 game turns into a 7–6 win for Cranbrook. But all parents from both teams stand. Both sides cheer and stamp and clap. After watching our kids lose all weekend, we've bonded over this bit of excitement. "Now *that* is a match," we say over and over again, high-fiving strangers. *Way to go, Cranbrook! Way to go, Fernie! Way to go, kids!*

A big dad from Cranbrook looks at me with tears in his eyes. His face jumps out of the sea of white, and I notice the Ktunaxa Nation badge on his leather jacket. "All right, Fernie," he says. "Best game all season! All right! *This* is how sport should be!"

I sense he'd be just as happy if the score had fallen 6–7 the other way. He cheers their effort, their heart. He cheers that it turned into a real game and that the kids played like they had something at stake.

We see the Ktuanxa dad again in the dressing room hallway, and I love his euphoric smile. I love his ability to celebrate fully. "Bring it in, Fernie," he says, opening his arms wide to me and Amanda. "Give me some love." He pulls us both into a hug, and we're all giddy with happiness. "Best game ever," he's still saying as he walks away. "Best game."

It's a beautiful, perfect hockey scene — a hug with a dad from the other side; the joy we take in effort alone — and in that moment, I love the sport. In that moment, I have no doubts at all about hockey.

• • •

Standing outside our own change room, waiting for the coach's call for us to come help the kids with their skates, the vibe changes. Jacob's mom is fuming. I try to remember her reaction during the two-team parental celebration. I can't. I work to catch her attention. "Is everything all right?" I feel like I need to say something. "Vivian? Are you okay?"

"No, I am not okay. And he is going to hear about it! The little brat. I did not come all this way to watch him play like that. He got moved to defense! Defense! He doesn't even know how to play defense. And when I cheered at him to *try harder,* he looked my way and shrugged. Cheek! Pure cheek! Well, we'll see how much cheek he has when I bench him next game. I'll bench him."

She has let her emotions get out of control, and everyone watches. It's hard to look away. She will be embarrassed later, when she's no longer intoxicated on anger. I recognize her as a nervous type who lets her feelings undo her. "He just had an off game," I tell her. "Everyone has an off game."

"Well, he's going to hear from me." Vivian crosses her arms tight around her body, eyes fixed on the change-room door. The other parents take a step back from her, exchange glances. The euphoria of the post-game celebration drains out of us.

And then the change room offers another microclimate all together. I can't keep up with the drastic changes in weather: euphoric, furious, ecstatic. That's sport too. Ollie levitates with happiness. His good friend, the littlest player on the team, has been awarded the golden jersey for Player of the Game.

"He's never got it before! And he didn't used to be good! But he's getting good now!"

Sharon has been quiet this season, tired of single-handedly taking on hockey culture. But I find out later that today's award is her doing. She complained about the golden jersey and the way it works to single out the best player in a team sport. She insisted that the post-game narrowing of focus to one player discourages those athletes always excluded. Sharon suggested, instead, that the coaches ensure each player get the golden jersey once and then put the jersey away to refocus the team's attention more productively and praise *everyone* for improvement and effort.

The award to this little player will be the jersey's last appearance for the year. Ollie didn't show nearly as much enthusiasm for his own golden-jersey nod at the start of the season. To see him so pleased for his friend makes my heart sing. I pat his head and pretend to be grossed out by the splash of sweat. I hold up the wet hand for a high five. "Good third period," I say. "You guys sure came to life." I try not to lie or give undeserved praise.

Ollie's so absorbed in celebrating his little friend's golden jersey that he's slow to get changed. I have to keep prompting him along: *chest pad off, elbow pads off, get it all in the bag, shin pads off, other shin pad too, c'mon, c'mon, c'mon.*

Gradually, Ollie comes out of his own enthusiasm to recognize what's going on beside him.

Vivian has charged into the room, her face inches from her son Jacob's face, her finger waving. She speaks loudly, but I've come to the conversation late and I don't catch everything.

"So disappointed!"

I hear that, a few times.

And then again: "Do not disappoint me like that again! EVER!"

Jacob looks slapped.

He does not cry, but Ollie does. Ollie looks as mortified as when I told him about the children taken away from their parents. At his age, every injustice is the same injustice, every digression from what is right, the same digression.

"His *mom* told him he didn't play well? His *MOM*? Why would she say that? She's making Jacob *sad*."

Immersed in her own anger, Vivian gives no indication of having heard Ollie. "I will talk to you more at home!" She's shaking as she barges out of the room. With her gone, Jacob does start crying. He is silent, but big tears stream down his elfin face.

"Oh, sweetie." I smile, taking his chin in my hand. I remember some rule about not touching other people's kids. I lift my other hand and wipe the tears from his cheek. "It's okay. Really. Your mom just got a bit too emotional. Remember: it's a game. Don't cry. Everything will be fine."

Jacob nods as I talk, and slowly his stunned expression softens and his tears dry, but he doesn't say a word.

Ollie, on the other hand, will not stop talking. "His mom!" Ollie holds both hands in the air, a baffled shrug, and shakes his head dramatically. His facial expression says pure tragedy.

"Ollie, please get your stuff in your bag and your clothes on your body. We'll talk about it in the car. Really. Ollie. Stop." I push him toward the equipment bag. "*We will talk about it in the car.*"

I'm so focused on Ollie and Jacob that I've barely taken in the rest of the room. I see now we're all jammed in here — parents and kids. Everyone witnessed the scene. The atmosphere has cooled again. Jacob's dad stands stoic near the door. He and the

176

mom have not been together for a long time, and I can't tell what he thinks of her parenting approach. In the stands, he tends to be one of the louder, more critical yellers. Maybe he agrees with her. I try to read him, wonder if I should say something, but he will not meet my eye. I want out of here. I've changed my mind about hockey again.

I hate it.

In the hallway, Amanda tells me that Jacob's dad is angry. Parents mutter about whether they should talk to the coaches. Who will talk to Vivian? Her behavior cannot be allowed to stand.

• • •

This awful moment in the hockey change room has freed me from the idea of a punishment approach to athletic performance. I look at the defeat, the utter empty discouragement on Jacob's face, and I know nothing positive will come from this scene.

Research supports my intuition. Anthony Vincent Battaglia, for example, wrote a 2015 dissertation on athletic punishment, considering the effectiveness of such discipline in relation to sport performance. He focused his research on hockey and defined punishment as "benching, yelling, and forced physical conditioning." In the end, he decided that though hockey normalizes these methods, they all have detrimental effects. He speculates that the prevalence of this type of discipline explains why hockey participation in Canada tends to decline from ten to thirteen years of age with youth athletes citing "lack of fun" and "coach conflicts" as common reasons for sport withdrawal. Every participant in his study knew at least one other athlete who had withdrawn from hockey participation because of this kind of punishment. He concludes, "Only when those in the sporting domain focus on youth athletes' developmental needs and growth-enhancing coaching methods, will an environment characterized by low attrition rates and healthy, holistic youth-athlete development be created."

177

In Ollie's words: *just be nice.* If coaches and parents cannot be nice, kids will not have fun. Kids who do not have fun will not stay in the sport. To draw my conclusions, I needed five minutes in that one hockey locker room with that one crying boy.

In the car, Ollie has calmed down and I escape the second-by-second rehash of the change-room horror. He says simply, "Can you not ever tell that to me? That I didn't try hard enough?"

Suddenly this question that I'd pondered in the stands with no resolution seems so very simple. I'm ashamed of myself for considering discipline, punishment, or threats. I suppose I want to think I have a job, and that there's something I can do to make Ollie better and to make our time at the arena more fulfilling and productive and, ultimately, to make him happier. Maybe the hardest thing for parents to do is nothing. "Yes, Ollie. I will never say that to you. I promise."

Ollie can decide how hard Ollie wants to try. After all my deliberation and reading and fretting, the best answer turns out to be the easiest answer — the answer that should have been obvious all along. Ollie's effort is up to Ollie.

CHAPTER TEN

ARE WE
THERE YET?

One tournament bleeds into the next, each game the same game. I can hardly tell them apart even as they're happening. They win some. They lose some. I find I don't care very much. I'm just glad Ollie's skates still fit. Am I in Cranbrook, Golden, Invermere, Whitefish, Kimberley? I don't even know. A rink is a rink is a rink is a rink. The coffee tastes just as old and bitter everywhere, my butt just as frozen and numb in this arena as in the last arena. I don't want to count the hours I spend on winter highways with Ollie in the backseat, carsick and complaining. Marty and I occasionally pass in the kitchen, blurs of fatigue. He hauls his exhausted body home from work just as I head off to hockey practice. By the time Ollie and I return, Marty's already sleep-walking through his pre-bed routine of checking the news (i.e., reading up on the Habs), making his lunch, and setting the coffee maker. On weekends, he bolts to the hill with Katie, and I'm off to another rink with Ollie. The only good news? We're never in the same room long enough for our sparks of annoyance to ignite into a truly raging fight. We are a family divided.

I myself am divided too. I carry an odd sorrow with me through my mundane routine, an empty ache disconnected from my day-to-day activities. I've never been one to cry over boys, but for weeks I weep over this one, a man I met three times, a man who was essentially my pen pal. My reaction strikes me as so unlikely that I look at my bloodshot eyes in the rearview mirror and think: they can't be my eyes. I don't do this. I barely know him. A doctor friend tells me my current condition has a medical term: "overfeel."

I overfeel.

Thank you, Doctor.

I go to the acupuncturist for my broken heart. "I lost a friend," I tell her, "and I'm so sad. Can you make me un-sad?" She tells me I have to let the emotion move. Stuck emotion creates pain. She pokes needles in my knees and my hands and my feet. In my forehead and my chest and my ears. I won't say it works, but when she takes the needles out, I feel better.

If pressed to explain my reaction, I suppose I mourn the hint of romance, the potential of passion and excitement. Sipping wine in hospitality suites, bathing in natural hot springs, lunching at remote mountain lodges, performing on grand stages for rapt audiences, flirting . . . *god flirting!* — all exist in a different galaxy than Planet Hockey. I miss that galaxy. I want to go there again, but I suspect I never will. So I cry, heartbroken.

But Atom hockey does not slow its wheels for my out-of-proportion, ridiculous grief. I wipe my eyes and drive on.

"Are you okay, Mom?"

"Yes, Ollie, I'm totally okay."

And I am. Kind of. I just want life to be better than *okay*.

This yearning for excitement, stimulation, passion stems partly from the athletic life. In *The Great Gatsby*, Fitzgerald describes Tom Buchanan, the novel's athlete, as "one of those men who reach such an acute limited excellence at twenty-one that everything afterward savors of anti-climax." I've seen this phenomenon in my most successful athlete friends. I've watched the disappointment of regular life.

And still I support — if not push — my kids into this same athletic existence. When we're not at the rink, we're at the pool. I've insisted both my children do one year of swimming but only in the moderate non-competitive stream. At the end of that year, I tell them, they will have an informed opinion of whether or not they like swimming and then they can decide if they wish to continue in the sport. Katie already shows interest in moving to three practices per week instead of two and attending some meets. Ollie, on the other hand, has put up quite a fight.

"You have to know how to swim, Ollie."

"I *know* how to swim."

"It's good for your lungs."

"I already have excellent lungs. Watch." He holds his breath until he loses color. He does one hundred jumping jacks without getting winded.

"You'll love swim racing."

"*I* love hockey. *You* can love swim racing if you want."

"The thing about swimming is it's no fun until you get good. Do it long enough to get good and then you can stay or leave. You wait and see: you'll thank me that you're a strong swimmer. You can be a lifeguard one day."

"You said kids' sports are like kids' marriages. Parents don't get to choose."

I talk too much, and Ollie listens too hard. "I didn't say that to you. You weren't supposed to be eavesdropping. Think of swimming as an arranged marriage. I know what's best." Only I find this funny.

"It's *not* fair."

"Swimming will be good cross-training. It'll make you better at hockey."

This gives him pause.

"For one year," he finally says. "*One* year. Then I get to decide. You *promised.*"

So he treks off to the pool, little sister in tow, with towel, swimsuit, and goggles stuffed in a grocery sack and slung over his shoulder, me a mush of nostalgia. *They're finally speed swimming!* But even at this recreational level, Ollie and I negotiate every single practice — more bribes, more promises, more threats, more arguments, more whining. By contrast, I realize, Ollie really does *want* to play hockey, and only hockey. Partly, I insist on swimming because I want him to have options in case he should decide to leave hockey. His December birthday will be no disadvantage in swimming where kids change age groups on their exact birthday, regardless when it falls.

But also experts recommend children do several sports into their teenage years. Children should not have narrowed to one sport by the age of ten. Overuse injuries are only one deterrent from specializing too young. Children who participate in many sports will become more well-rounded athletes. They can benefit from the footwork of soccer, the hand-eye coordination of tennis, the flexibility of gymnastics, the teamwork skills of hockey, and the strength and full-body awareness of wrestling, all without growing bored or injuring themselves. Dividing their time in this way will avoid the early burnout that's becoming more common right alongside early specialization.

A 2014 Sportsnet article complained that the rest of the world had caught up to Canada in hockey, partly because of the early specialization. Experts argue competitive hockey should be delayed to age twelve like in European countries, and children should instead be encouraged to participate in many sports at a recreational level. Michael Grange wrote the article in response to

Canada's lack of hockey dominance at the 2014 Winter Olympics at a time that Canada led the world with 2,631 indoor rinks and with the 625,152 players using those rinks. In comparison, Sweden had only 353 rinks and 64,214 players (about twenty-three percent fewer bodies competing for ice time, proportionally). In light of these statistics, even the Swedish coaches found it absurd that Sweden could pull together a team that could beat Canada at an international level. Michael Grange gave a straight-forward, simple answer to his question "Why isn't Canada more dominant in hockey?" Too specialized too young.

Buoyed by expert opinions, I won't let Ollie make the decision to forego swimming and all other sports to focus solely on hockey, certainly not yet. But a series of events confirm that I did make the right choice when I decided to follow Ollie's lead about how much effort he wants to invest in hockey and to relieve myself of the job of pushing him. When I think back to the start of the season and his intuitive decision to skip A-team tryouts, I feel pure gratitude and relief.

First, on February 18th, Oliver's team gets invited to play ball hockey on television for CBC's "Hockeyville in Canada" in Cranbrook, B.C. The children get instructions to dress head-to-toe in clothes plastered with the sponsor's logo.

Their sponsor? *McDonald's.*

I wish child sport didn't have to be about branding and massive corporations, and I'm especially uneasy when the product of a corporate sponsor is so directly at odds with the lifestyle and values supposedly upheld by amateur sport (i.e., health, well-being, fitness). But I know — it's TV, Ron MacLean will be there, it will be a big deal. I will hold my breath, plug my nose, and prepare to go.

But not one of the kids on Ollie's team wants to go.

"Why would we drive one hundred kilometers to play ball hockey for an hour? That seems silly." Ollie scrunches up his nose in confusion. *Adults! The ridiculous ideas they dream up!* "We can play ball hockey right in our own street without driving anywhere."

None of his teammates seem to care about the logos or the hoopla or the television or the celebrities, and none of their parents bother to push them. We don't go. Simple. *Hello, ski hill!*

The A-team players, however, don their corporate logos, enthusiastically showing up for the TV cameras, drawing my attention to a difference in attitude between the two teams, something that goes beyond skill level.

The contrasting parental mindsets come into clearer focus as a late-season controversy erupts. Going through the lobby after Ollie's practice, I sense an ugly tension. The parents stand close to each other in animated conversation, matching angry lines worried deep into their foreheads. They whisper so that I can't make out every word, but the meanness of their mouths and the tension in their shoulders tell me everything. I want to say, *Relax! Whatever has you so agitated — they're ten-year-olds. They play a game. It's meant to be fun. Go do some yoga.*

I recall grumpiness around the same time last year too, mostly fatigue induced. Each year, the A team goes to a tournament in Osoyoos, a six-hour drive each way. Some kids travel all that way to sit on the bench. "You know what that does at this age," Roland says. "Sends kids a message: 'You were not born good enough.' Kids who are better at this age are better because they've had more ice time. Giving them even more ice time only further disadvantages kids who need to catch up." I assume the parental anger this time has to do with this same kind of imbalance.

I'm wrong.

This time, parents complain not about some kids getting less ice time. The complaint is that the coaches have been playing the kids too equally.

Too. Equally. I get bits and pieces of the conversation and learn that the A-team parents have pushed out my favorite coach, the one who is smart, kind, sensitive, and fair. Russell started the season wanting to improve the hockey program in Fernie. He did research. He insisted the Atom A and Atom B teams practice together once a week. He put them through the same circuit of drills, focusing on developing the same skills. He emphasized that fun and skill development should be the priority at this level, not competition. He also tried to tell people about the same conclusions I have been reading in youth-sport research — age ten is too early to single out "good" players for special treatment, too early to even know who the "good" players will be.

Now with the end of the season in sight, many of the A-team parents do not like Russell's approach. At this level, the rules specify that all kids must get equal ice time, but there is a "play to win" rule for the last five minutes in a tight game. A coach can bench the poor players and send out his good players in an attempt to get that final winning goal. Russell has never used that option. He always plays all children equally until the end. The parents who take exception to the A and B teams practicing together have also taken exception to Russell's "play to lose" attitude. Emotion escalates. They gang up on Russell. They speak behind his back. They rally support, call a venomous meeting. Ultimately, Russell feels compelled to submit his resignation. He continues to watch the games, but he doesn't sit with the other parents. He slouches at the boards, ostracized. He wants only for his son to be able to play, unaffected by the controversy.

The coup comes at the hands of some of the kindest and most involved parents. They seem — outside of the rink — like grounded, sensible people. Of the group leader, I ask another coach, "She's not one of those delusional parents who thinks her son will make the NHL, is she? Is that where this hypercompetitive drive comes from? And if not there, where?"

"No," the coach tells me, "she said she knows he won't make the NHL, that he's likely too small. But she said, 'He could be a star thirteen-year-old. That would be fun. What's wrong with wanting that for him?'"

So she wants her son to be a thirteen-year-old hockey star, and Russell, with his bizarre ideas of equality and skill development, stands in the way of that chance. She wants her son to get more ice time, even if it means benching other ten-year-olds, even if it means sending those players the message that they are a liability to their team, even if it means hurting kids' feelings. She wants her son to score goals and win, now. She's never played nor coached hockey, but she's pretty sure Russell's doing it wrong.

• • •

Russell, like all Atom hockey coaches across the country, is a *volunteer*. On his own time, he researched best hockey-coaching practices and how those best practices differ from typical Atom programs that focus too early on excellence, competition, and winning. In wanting to focus on skills rather than competition, in wanting to avoid hierarchical separation of the kids, Russell is at the cutting edge of the current research. He is far ahead of common hockey-programming practices in rural Canada. The A-team parents want no part of it. They want to win.

In pushing that desire, they lose a good volunteer who cares about all the players.

I'm relieved to be with the B team, but the kids sure do continue to play poorly. They lose 8–0 to a team they beat at the tiering tournament. Ollie's play is lackluster, and he occasionally erupts into frustration. In one particularly memorable shift, he makes his way down the ice, fighting Quinn for the puck.

"Ollie, you and Quinn are on the same team!" I pinch the bridge of my nose. "God, this is painful to watch," I mutter more quietly.

I hate parents who yell. I have become a parent who yells.

Suddenly, the negative energy in the stands reminds me of the A-team ugliness that I witnessed in the lobby. I've read all about the risk of player burnout, but around me I see *parent* burnout.

As another puck zooms by our goalie, a dad throws himself back in his seat and huffs, "Well, at least the goalie gets good practice when his team's so shitty." The discouraged dad has dark curls down to his shoulders and an oversized ball cap. Both his cap and his smile have a cocky tilt.

Vivian glares at him. He takes no notice of her, but the Cranbrook incident taught me something of her body language. I see the same edginess, the muscles tense in her neck, a nervous swing in her foot, her arms crossing and uncrossing. Vivian has apologized since her change-room outburst, for making Jacob cry. He'd been acting like a teenager, she said. His cheekiness surprised her. She overreacted. I understand, I told her. I also have a tendency to get emotional and nothing brings it on with more intensity than sport. I see her fury at this man who criticizes the kids, and I know she has a good, open heart. She feels deeply.

Vivian turns on the Atom heckler fast. "Did you say what I just heard you say?" Vivian shoves his knee when he ignores her. "You! Did you really say that? Are you fucking kidding me?"

The dad throws his head back and holds a hand to his heart in mock shock at her attack and then turns to his friend, laughing. His laughter excludes her. *Women, what do they know?*

"You say you're sorry!" Vivian's volume rises. "To the kids and then to the parents! How dare you call them shitty? How dare you!"

"I'm not apologizing," the man tells her, shrugging at the friend and rolling his eyes, easily dismissing Vivian's outburst. "There's no trophies for last. It's sport."

"Yep, they've gotta learn," his friend agrees. "People are going to say to them: you're leaving your goalie out to dry. You're playing like shit."

"And that mom," the dad says as if Vivian's not listening, "is going to have to get a thicker skin. It's hockey."

It's hockey. A phrase invoked to excuse so much misbehavior, immaturity, insensitivity, and unkindness.

• • •

The parents continue to bicker in the stands as the final seconds of the game grunt to a halt. In the change room, I find Ollie nearly in tears. He says he got pulled off the ice for trying to take the puck from Quinn and it's not fair because Quinn was hogging the puck and anyways Quinn never gets pulled off when he takes the puck from someone and maybe it's because Quinn's dad is coach and why doesn't Ollie get to play just as much as Quinn and . . . *oh my god will this season never end?*

While Ollie rants to me, one of the coaches hands out coupons for a free ice-cream cone. He runs out just before he gets to Ollie, a crisis that tops all the day's other crises.

"I'll buy you an ice cream, Ollie. It doesn't matter."

Ollie becomes incoherent and I know the look on his face — he's tired and he's hungry and he's inconsolable.

"Ollie, go to the lobby. Take your bag. Settle yourself down. I'm going to talk to the coach for a minute."

"So." I tap on the coach's shoulder. These locker rooms are inhospitable to women. I know a father would be taken more seriously in this context. I envy the women who know their children have a coach-parent on the bench. Ollie doesn't have that kind of advocate. I don't want to be "that parent," but if anyone will speak up for Ollie, it will have to be me. "So at this age," I ask tentatively, "all the kids get equal ice time, right?"

"Absolutely!" The coach looks at me with big eyes, the image of sincerity. "We do our best. Sometimes kids fly on and off the ice, and things move fast and we might give one kid a longer shift than another. But we hope those small differences even out over a season."

"Ollie felt like he got pulled off today and that some of the other kids are getting more ice time. But I know — he gets over-emotional and he has been getting a bit frustrated as the season goes on." I'm nervous now that I have the coach's attention and I don't even know what I'm complaining about. I remember Coach Bub kicking me out of the change room at the start of the season, and I resolve to stand strong and say my bit. "Do you remember that conversation we had about six games ago? You and I both noticed Ollie plays better when he plays center — he doesn't think so intently and worry about getting out of position and he can just chase the puck hard — and you were going to let him play center . . ." I stop. What do I know about hockey? What am I saying? What differentiates me from the moms complaining that Russell's coaching style isn't competitive enough? Who asked for my coaching advice? "And . . . well, Ollie hasn't played center since you said that, and we only have one tournament left and I'm wondering if maybe he can play center."

"Oh! Totally, Ang! I completely forgot. All these kids. You're right — I did say that and Ollie plays great at center. Like his head's on fire. Next game. For sure. I promise."

We high-five, and it's that easy. The coach finds an extra ice-cream coupon (though I will wonder afterward if he took it from his own child). I thank him for his volunteer work and tell him I appreciate his great contribution and kindness to the kids. He thanks me for reminding him of his idea about Ollie playing center. It's the way a coach-parent relationship should be. I can make reasonable requests, and the coach can respond reasonably. Mothers do not need to be excluded. They can be allowed to act as advocates for their own children in sensible and measured ways. We can model this clear, direct, and non-sexist communication as an example to the children on the team — the girls and the boys.

If I were the dad, I could have just said, "Hey, man, what do you think of giving Ollie a shot at center?" And the coach would've said, "Sure, man, no problem." Coach-parent communication should work the same for mothers and fathers because, to steal a phrase from Justin Trudeau, *it's 2017!* But it doesn't always feel like 2017 in the hockey locker room. Hockey's got some catching up to do.

• • •

"The coach is going to let you play center next weekend," I tell Ollie in the car.

"Hmmph." He slumps in his seat.

"You're still mad? About what?"

"I didn't get any goals and I hardly got the puck. It's like I don't even get a chance some games."

"You know what? When I swam, I had lots of bad races. All athletes do. And when you grow up, you'll have bad days at work or bad days in your relationships. What you could try to do is learn something from the bad games and then let them go. You know what I mean? Holding onto it like you are now doesn't do anything except make you feel yucky. It for sure won't help you play better next time."

He shrugs. "Yeah, I guess."

"And at least you played your hardest."

"Mom?"

"Yeah, Ollie?"

"No, I didn't." He scrunches up his face, ashamed of his own confession. "I didn't play my hardest."

This confession shocks me — he's only a kid, but he knows. I think of all the ways adults lie to themselves about their own behavior and push blame elsewhere. I'm surprised at his self-perception, his honesty. "You have no idea how proud I am of you, Ollie. For admitting that you didn't try your hardest, not only admitting it to me, which doesn't matter much, but admitting it to yourself. That's huge."

He's sprouted over the season. His height disorients me. He has lost all his baby teeth too. I see now his growth extends beyond the physical.

"Even that, what you just said, is a lesson of sport," I tell him. "One of the best lessons. Maybe that's the reason you didn't like this game. Hockey feels better when you try your hardest, anything does."

"I'm going to try my hardest next time." He nods, determined. He fills his voice with such conviction that I am sure he will.

• • •

Maybe if we focus on the lessons of sport, we can be less defined by the so-called failures. Glen Belfry, my university swim coach, always said the successful athlete must have three things: 1) talent, 2) work ethic, and 3) luck. Glen used Canadian swimmer Joanne Malar as an example. Qualifying for her first Olympic trials at age twelve, Malar obviously had talent. She didn't rest on that alone, though. Legend has it that nobody worked like her. At McMaster University, people gathered in the stands to watch her train. Not only did she swim with the men, but she often led the lane. And then luck plays an important role too. Everything has to line up for those big competitions: health, taper, natural peak, right venue, right time of day. For Joanne, her best showings never coincided with Olympic events. Despite a long and tremendously impressive career (as well as a prime spot on the nation's Kellogg's boxes in the lead-up to the 2000 Games), Joanne Malar ended her swimming days without an Olympic medal. Despite her many years of international swimming success, when someone asks her, "Did you win an Olympic medal?" She must answer, "No."

I bet she has had days — or even years — when that no defined her.

• • •

Just as I'm plotting my escape from hockey, begging the time clock to tick down the final seconds of this season, Ollie gets his mojo back. He's keen to go to every practice. He's happy afterward, chatting about the drills and the scrimmages and the jokes with his coaches. He clicks with his teammates, makes new friends.

"I love that new drill," he says. "It's really tiring. But it's awesome." He's proud of himself when his muscles ache, when he works up a two-burger appetite, when he skates so hard he falls fast asleep by eight thirty. Everything seems quiet on the school front too. His happiness makes me happy. Simple.

But nobody can be happy all the time.

I remember a rough spot in my life, between marriages. I had left a husband my parents liked. While figuring out my personal life, I also dropped out of a PhD program when I should have been graduating and competing for a faculty position. I went from calling my mom almost daily to being unavailable for weeks. When they did manage to get me on the phone, I came across as uncommunicative and surly. I remember feeling my parents wanted me to "perform happy." I'm just living my life, I thought, I don't want an audience. Not all the time.

In being so intent to give Ollie an audience, I forgot that parental spectating too requires balance. I've been watching too closely, too much. I need to look away now and then to give him a break from my gaze, from the performance it requires of him. Looking away will give him a chance to figure out independently who he wants to be and what he wants to do. Released from the expectation inherent in my gaze, he can simply *play*. He can relax into himself without the relentless questions implied by my constant watching.

Is he happy? Is he good? Is he happy? Is he good? Does he love hockey? Does he love hockey? Does he love hockey?

But does he *love* it?

I'm exhausting.

• • •

You don't watch me enough.

You watch me too much.

Getting the balance right feels like an impossible challenge. For direction, I have started to look more often to John O'Sullivan and his Changing the Game Project. O'Sullivan complains that parents have claimed their children's youth sport experience for themselves. He proves his point by highlighting our pronoun usage: *we won, we lost, we scored, we went into overtime, we played badly.*

Why we? It's *they* won or lost. *They* scored. *They* played well or badly. *We* merely spectate. O'Sullivan warns against this vicarious approach to sport and points to a groundbreaking Dutch study that discovered parents who see their children as extensions of themselves tend to expect the children to live out the parents' unfulfilled athletic dreams. We must let our children be themselves, separate from us, and live their own lives. O'Sullivan continually reminds parents that three key ingredients make up positive youth sport experience: ownership of the game, enjoyment of the game, and intrinsic motivation to play. Parents do not make athletes. O'Sullivan takes a phrase from Bruce Brown, founder of Proactive Coaching, and encourages parents to "release their children to the game."

We in the stands should not coach or correct or instruct. We should not evaluate. We should sit quietly and watch. When the game ends, we should say, "I love watching you play." That's all. With alarm, I read O'Sullivan's suggestion that by doing more than that, we force our kids to feel responsible for our happiness. If a child sees his parent looking angry or disappointed because of a loss — or elated because of a victory — that child takes on the burden of the parent's well-being. No child should be responsible for a mother or father's happiness.

Sometimes we parents can look away, let the kids muck around for a bit unobserved, figure out who they are, what they want, and how to get it.

Ollie and his teammates have only one tournament left, the final banner tournament in Invermere. For it, I will release Ollie to the game.

"I love to watch you play, Ollie."

I will say only that, and I will mean it.

CHAPTER ELEVEN

LET'S PLAY

"But what would you say to parents who want to know how to support their children in sport? Parents who want to know if they even should support swimming goals or hockey goals or soccer goals? Or if maybe those things are, like, kind of a waste of time?"

I'm doing a guest lecture at Nipissing University's Sport Literature course. The students have recently read my novel *The Bone Cage*. I often find humor in these questions, when audiences direct them toward other fiction writers. It's funny to me that readers think we have these answers. We're novelists. We make up stories. Madeleine Thien wrote a novel about the aftermath of the Tiananmen Square massacre, and I've seen audiences ask her questions that would be more appropriately directed toward the world's foremost political leaders. At least my readers only ask me about sport.

I want to tell this student she can find everything I know, exactly as I know how to say it, within the pages of *The Bone Cage*. Fiction writing allows me to be a little cryptic in my responses. "Novelists don't have to give direct answers," I say. "Novels allow the interplay of many perspectives. Novels start the conversation but then allow readers to figure out where they fit within the multi-vocal response to any issue." See that — how I can hide behind language? I have fancy ways of saying *I don't know. I'm not sure.* Normally at this point, I would redirect the question back to the student. "What responsibility do *you* think parents have to their children-athletes?"

But now I'm writing a nonfiction book, and the student has posed the *exact* question I *should* be able to answer. Nonfiction writers should have answers — direct ones, not metaphors and allusions and analogies.

How would I advise parents who want to support their children in sport?

I didn't know the answer when I started writing this book, but I embarked upon the project to find my answer.

"It's a good question," I say to buy myself some time. The young woman who asked plays hockey, like my Ollie. Her dad drove her year after year to every local practice and around the province to every tournament. Eventually, as she made her way to national-level competition, those commuting obligations turned to airfares. The financial commitment increased, but her father never wavered. However, while he supported her passion for hockey unconditionally, her mother rolled her eyes and asked her when she would grow up and do something real.

"I know my book seems critical of sport," I say, "of the level of sacrifice, the damage to the body, the media's emphasis on Olympic medals, the broken dreams, broken hearts. But anyone who reads my physical descriptions of swimming and wrestling will know that I *love* sport. I guess chasing an athletic dream is like falling in love." I'm making it up as I go at this point. The Nipissing students will know my answer at the same time as I do. "I would never stand in the way of love. If I tried, I would fail. Any parent who has tried to throw up obstacles to a child's love affair knows that. The parents lose, always. But I wouldn't push my children toward romance either, or even encourage it. There will be so much pain! That's true in both love and sport. What mother wants to see her child in pain?" I have the students' attention, if only because they think I'm completely mad. Or maybe they can tell I'm off script and what I'm saying is truer than what I intended to say.

"My friend Andy worked so hard at swimming. He's that guy who never missed a practice, whose face went blazing red every set. He never made it to the Olympics. He never even made it to national championships. For decades, he didn't see the sense of the work he put into swimming. It felt like a failed relationship: all give and no take. In his thirties, he said swimming broke his heart. Now in his forties, he loves swimming again. He's happiest when he's moving through the water. He feels good. He's realized he can't measure the rewards of swimming in national time standards and podium appearances. Mark Tewksbury had the Olympic success every athlete dreams of, but he had the same experience of despair at the end of his athletic career. I heard Tewksbury speak shortly after he won Olympic gold and he said, 'The Olympics leaves its athletes broken souls.' If athletes expect validation via medals, their experience of sport will be disappointing, whether or not they reach the podium. And maybe an athletic career always ends with a broken heart. It's the end of a relationship after all — a relationship to which you devote more time and energy than you will to most other relationships in your life." I look into the crowd of pixelated Skype faces. Through the computer screen, I can't tell if the Nipissing University students are still with me. At this point, I might as well be alone in my office talking to myself. "So maybe we should ask: why would a parent support something that, in the end, will break the child's heart? But that's life. We can't put our kids under a bell jar either. If you live fully, if you enthusiastically throw yourself into endeavors and relationships, you *will* break your heart. But to live with your heart protected — that's not living."

If I had my years of youth to do over again, I would swim. For sure, I would. No hesitation. The sport gave me so much joy. It still does. That's my heart's true answer, and I will never be able to say no to a child's heart. As long as Ollie wants to play hockey, as long as he's choosing with *his* heart, I will do everything I can to support him.

One of Ollie's coaches grew up in a Hutterite colony. He and his friends played pond hockey in every spare moment. The teachers didn't like the language the boys used during their heated games. When the boys seemed unable to curb their cursing, the German teacher confiscated their hockey skates, piled them high in the middle of the colony, and burned them to the ground. What did the boys do? They waited for the ashes to cool, pulled the blades from the wreckage, taped them to their shoes, and kept right on playing. Maybe I couldn't stop hockey even if I wanted to.

In *King Leary*, one of my favorite hockey novels, Paul Quarrington writes that hockey didn't originate. It's always just been there, like the moon. Ollie laughs when I read him this passage: *like the moon!* But then he adds, "Hey, when *did* I start hockey? I don't remember my first time." In Ollie's ten years, hockey *has* always been there. I feel the same about swimming: it's always been in my life, like the moon. I'm grateful my own son will have the same kind of grounding activity that brings him back to the strength and speed and power of his body, back to joy in physical movement, and back to a love of childlike play. I hope hockey does that for him. If it does, who cares how many gold medals he wins? Who cares how good he is? Those who play for a true love of sport measure success in a different currency.

• • •

With everything falling into place at hockey — with Ollie trying hard and making friends and coming home from every practice with his face full of pure exhilaration — his report card comes as a dropkick to my gut. We haven't heard a peep from the school since the last semester's report card and parenting meeting. Things improved after we left Hockey Academy last year. He slid back into some troubling behavior with the adjustment to grade four, but all has appeared well and calm since Christmas. Now, in March, we learn otherwise. My son has not been happy and relaxed at school. I'd nearly forgotten this version of Ollie that his teachers describe in the fifteen single-spaced pages of that report card. Frustrated, quick to tears, overblown meltdowns, inability to complete work. His failure to handle his emotions, the reports tell me, threatens to stigmatize him with his peers.

Oh no. I turn to another page packed full of discouraging news. *No, no, no.*

If a boy seems so very unhappy, why wouldn't someone tell his parents? We had thought things were going better now that we were out of the Hockey Academy. The school had promised us clear communication, but we must wait until report card season to learn that our son cries almost every day?

We need a new start. He needs a place that will see the good in him, nurture his creativity. Let him be himself. He does not fit into the tight square box this school has for him, just as he did not fit into its hockey program.

Marty and Ollie have both been resisting change to a new school, but armed with the nastiness of this report card and the lack of clear and helpful communication since the previous report card, I try again.

But Marty and I have hardly seen each other all season. When we do, we negotiate schedules and stress over bills. We have not been acting like friends, let alone lovers. We have been snappy and unkind. The friction makes it difficult to talk about anything that really matters.

"Let's just go to the parent-teacher interview and see what they say," Marty suggests. He prides himself on being less reactive than me.

"I've seen what they say. I've sat at that table across from those people too many times. They promise one thing and do another. They told me he would be seeing a counselor for his anxiety. Now I learn she stopped seeing him. You know *why* the counselor stopped seeing Ollie? Because being pulled out of the class away from the other students caused him anxiety. She was treating him for *anxiety* and stopped because he was *anxious*? And nobody even *told* us? I thought they were helping him and . . ."

I know I'm ranting. My words pick up speed like they're rolling downhill. They gather anger as they go. Marty will receive that anger as if it's directed at him. He never responds well when I get emotional. He hears it as a lecture.

"I'm done with this school. Ollie needs a new start. He needs people who will see the good in him and help him control his emotions and keep us informed."

"I will go to the parent-teacher interview and see what they say." There's a razor edge to Marty's words, one I know well. Our conversation has come to its end.

"Okay. I'm not coming. Not this time. I'm finished."

• • •

Marty returns from that interview charged up. They've got plans! Ideas! "We're all on the same side," he says. "We'll get this under control."

Marty pulls out his little notepad and flips through pages filled with his tiny script. Like me, he's trying hard. He tells me that Ollie's principal and teacher want Ollie to put extra time into school work. Ollie will do better if he has some quiet hours where he can work on his studies uninterrupted. The solution? Ollie can stay at school in the evenings, instead of swimming or hockey.

"It'll be a better use of his time," Marty says.

I don't say anything because Marty and I don't always communicate well. When we disagree, we fight. I'm not up for that, but, boy, do I disagree.

I picture Ollie coming home from school, angry and grumpy, throwing his backpack on the floor and complaining about the day, edgy and cantankerous. He's like his dad and me. He needs physical activity to keep happy. I picture him coming home from swimming and hockey: "That drill was so hard but it was awesome!" I see his flushed, healthy face; I hear his elated chatter. The pride he takes in his work pleases me. His smile makes me smile. That's the state I want my son to be in, as much as he can.

This new idea — more school work and less physical activity — does not sit well with me.

I have the sinking feeling that Ollie's childhood has taken a wrong turn. Grade four should not be stressful.

He can't play? He can't exercise?

No. I will not let this happen.

Ollie and I set off to the final banner tournament, and I have one goal: convince Ollie he wants to change schools.

Amanda and I have decided to make this last hockey trip a girls' weekend. Roland stays home with the dogs. Marty stays home with Katie. Amanda and I rent a condo in Invermere and fill the van to the roof with hockey equipment and groceries. As she drives, I read her my text messages from the school's principal.

"What?" Amanda's shock mirrors my own, but she laughs. With Amanda, even outrage is fun. "He's *already* in school seven hours a day. What can't they do in seven hours a day?"

I'm grateful for this affirmation of the craziness of the suggestion. Too often, I waffle about parenting. I feel fraudulent, wondering who granted me all this power. How am I supposed to know what's best for a little human being? But this time I *know* I'm right.

I watch Ollie chatter in the back of the van with Amanda's two kids — what great plays they're going to make, how many goals they will score, what super awesome games they will invent in the pool afterward — and I know *this* is what Ollie needs.

"Hey," I shout over my shoulder to Amanda's children, "you guys like the public school, right?"

"Why? Is Ollie going to change? Are you going to change, Ollie?" Grady's freckled face fills with a smile at the thought.

But Ollie hesitates. There's a strong rivalry between the two schools, and he's spent the last five years convincing himself the Academy is best. "I don't know," he says. "A lot of my friends go to the Academy. And I'm kind of used to it and . . ."

"You have lots of friends at the other school too," I remind him. "These guys go to the other school. Half your hockey team will be in your class."

"We have a basketball team at our school," Grady offers.

"Mmm. I don't really like basketball." Ollie twists his fingers. Even the idea of change makes him anxious.

"There's a cross-country running team," Grady's sister tries.

"I think I get enough exercise with hockey," Ollie says, polite but firm.

Grady's little sister watches the boys for a few minutes as they ping-pong back and forth, Grady selling the public school and Ollie striking him down. She leans forward in her seat. "You really want him to switch to the public school, don't you?"

"I really do," I say. "I think he'll be happier."

"Hey, Ollie," she says leaning back in her seat. "We get out-door recess."

"Outdoor recess?!" Ollie sounds like she's just offered him a trip to Disneyland.

"Twice a day," she adds with a smug smile. She knows she's won.

"Outdoor recess!" He looks at me like I've been keeping something from him. "*Outdoor* recess! *I* want to go to the public school."

"Done," I exclaim from the front seat. I meet Amanda's high five and then I'm texting Marty: "Ollie wants to switch schools. We'll save a bunch of money. You can get new skis."

Within seconds, I get my response: "SOLD! 👍😊"

New skis and outdoor recess? These guys. I've been taking the wrong approach all along.

Before we get to Invermere, I've already spoken with the new principal, the new teacher, and the new guidance counselor. Ollie has decided he doesn't want to wait until spring break to switch. He wants to change schools on Monday. Even from my short conversations with the school staff, I know this move will be exactly what he needs. Less pressure, less rigid ideas of how he should be, less stress. The new teacher will appreciate his strengths and gently help him to work on his challenges. She will encourage his creativity and he will thrive under her appreciative eye.

In a month's time, his new teacher will look at me with tears in her eyes. "I read that Academy report card, and *I* have some feedback for *them*. I couldn't believe it. I wanted to hug Ollie and say, 'You know this report card is *not* you, right?'"

I will love her — because she sees my son. She nurtures the best in him instead of exacerbating the worst.

• • •

We pull into Invermere fired up. Maybe the kids are just excited about their last tournament or maybe they pick up on the energy of positive and immediate change. Amanda pats me on the back as we get out of the van, the boys running ahead, dragging their oversized equipment bags, sticks swinging over their shoulders. I've taken that photograph so often: my son's back, Ollie No. 11, carrying everything he needs and venturing off without me.

"This change will be good," Amanda says.

The enthusiasm carries through the games. The coach makes good on his promise to let Ollie play center. Ollie doesn't stress about getting out of position. He simply plays the puck. He's right on it every shift, at his best.

I love watching him play, just like O'Sullivan says, I really do.

Their first day's games all end close. They lose 6–4. They win 10–8. They get up. They get down. In the stands, we lean forward, hands clasped, watching every move, willing the clock to run faster when they're up and praying for it to slow down when they get behind.

Give them time, give them time, give them time.

Hurry up, hurry up, hurry up.

But no matter what the result — win or lose — the kids pour off the ice happy.

"You're right, Mom. Hockey *is* more fun when I try my hardest."

• • •

But what goes up must come down. We start Saturday morning with a crash. I'm feeling guilty because it's Katie's birthday. I will miss my daughter's eighth birthday for a hockey tournament. Marty and I need to think of a better strategy. Our divide-and-conquer method has its limitations. I can't miss everything of importance to Katie. Nor can I go months barely seeing my husband.

The morning game starts rough. The ref has his hands full, throwing kids into the penalty box. When he puts his hands on Ollie, though, I know we will have trouble. It will be a travesty of justice. It will be the end of the world. It will be *unfair!*

Ollie's crying before he even gets to the box. He throws his hands up, staring open mouthed into the crowd. *"What?! What?!"* Everything matters to Ollie. It's both his weakness and his strength.

"Jeez, Ollie, it's just a penalty," Quinn yells from the ice. "Relax."

The moms laugh because Quinn would say that — for the amount of time Quinn spends in the penalty box, he should pay rent. I laugh with the other parents, but I'm uneasy.

Ollie slams his stick as he heads into the box. The team dad working the door pats him on the shoulder, but Ollie angrily shrugs him off. Even from here, I can tell Ollie's a snot-covered mess.

Amanda puts her hand on my knee. "He'll be okay, mama."

The dad tries to talk Ollie down, but I can see he's escalating. I chew my knuckle. I know I could calm him down, but moms are not welcome at the penalty box. If Ollie doesn't calm down soon, he'll ruin his whole game. Things do not need to go this far off course.

"Just go," Amanda says, reading my mind. "Give him a little pep talk. Don't worry about it. They're just kids. Seeing his mom will help."

"Hey, Ollie." I rap on the glass. "Look at me. It's fine. You're playing hard, tough. You're going to get penalties. It's no big deal."

The dad shrugs at me, sympathetic. "I told him: he's playing great," he says. "Just go back out there, I told him, and make it up. Keep working hard." But Ollie won't look at either of us. If I didn't care so much about this boy of mine, the extreme anger and distress on his face would be comical. It's so vastly out of proportion.

When I spot the referee skating in my direction, I talk faster. I know he's on his way to send me off. "Ollie, just look at my eyes. It's okay." If I can get Ollie to connect with me, he'll calm down. The ref pounds the glass twice hard and points at me to go away.

I scurry. Exactly as I scurried at the start of the season, in response to Coach Bub's head wave. The universal message to hockey moms: "*Git!*"

"Did you see that baby ref?" I joke as I rejoin the parents. I feel sick, in truth, but I make light of it because I'm embarrassed. I've been reprimanded by a teenager. He doesn't know anything about Ollie and he has no business chasing a parent away from a ten-year-old boy in a recreational hockey game.

Ollie doesn't recover during the game. When he lines up to shake hands, he looks agitated. I don't run to the glass like I did at the end-of-season game last year. I've gotten myself in enough trouble for one day. I sit tight in my seat and watch my son cry.

· · ·

In the dressing room he's a sputtering mess. I tell him again and again that he played well and I'm proud of him. I tell him the penalty does not matter. He won't listen to me, won't even hold my eyes. I call Sharon over to talk to him. Really, I just want her to say "bullshit" to him. *That call was bullshit!* A teacher saying bullshit will make Ollie laugh. Laughter will fix everything.

Instead, Sharon gets down on her knee and looks him in the eye. "You listen to me, Ollie." He does. Her voice carries a teacher's authority. "You have improved so much this year. You're not even my son, and *I* am proud of you. You played so tough this game. That referee called too many penalties. We saw that. Maybe he shouldn't have called that one on you. Maybe you were just going hard for the puck like you're supposed to. But he put you in the box. And you know what? You're upset. And that's okay. You're upset because you care. You're upset because of what you have here." She puts a finger to his chest. "A big heart. That's what you have. And we all love you for it."

And now I'm crying along with Ollie because Sharon can see it too, Ollie's heart. I love her for seeing past the tears to what so many people miss.

As we leave the dressing room, I mutter, "If his skill ever catches up to his heart, the other team is in trouble."

Sharon knows I'm making a joke to take the edge off my emotion. She puts her arm around me in a tight hug. "You've got a good boy there, Ang."

I'm going to miss these crazy hockey moms.

For the final game, the kids come out with their heads ablaze.

It's fireworks for the whole three periods. Pure energy. The parents yell their throats hoarse. If I cared more about hockey, I'd write out the plays in full poetic detail. I'd make you see the way the players connected each pass with a sharp whack of their sticks. I'd show the beauty of their cross-over strides, their dekes, their pucks flying into the net's upper-left corner with a sweet whoosh. I'd let you hear the heavy thump of them going hard to the boards, pushing and grunting until they came out with the puck — then snapping it fast to a friend with that satisfying *whap* of connection. Mostly, I'd capture the way they've grown, the miracle of a pack of puck-chasing kids turning into a real hockey team in the space of a few short months.

But I don't really care about hockey. I care about Ollie.

In an introduction to Bill Gaston's hockey memoir, Will Ferguson writes that hockey is "cold fire. Steel on ice. It's chess played at two hundred miles an hour." I won't say I see that in these boys, not yet, but I do see its potential.

• • •

My heart sinks when partway through the third period Ollie gets a penalty. He turns slowly on his blade, finding my eyes in the stands. He gives me one quick nod. *No biggie*, the nod says, *I've got this.*

My eyes water.

"That's your superpower," I'll tell him later. "You learn fast. You took what Sharon said and put it into action just like that."

When his penalty runs out, he flies from the box faster than ever, straight for the puck. From the stands, we watch mouths agape as he makes his way down the ice, shoots, and scores. His eyes find me in the stands. He won't blow me a kiss, but I blow him one.

"Did you see that?" I say to Sharon. "After the travesty of this morning. It's that easy?"

"This morning needed to happen first," Sharon says. "Learning is messy."

Yes, learning can be messy, and in a two-day hockey tournament, Ollie learned more about managing and channeling his emotions than he learned in five years of school. I'm not taking him out of hockey for anything.

Sharon tells me that her son likely won't play next year. "He's thinking of doing a year of free skiing instead. He says he might come back to hockey, but he won't — not after he gets a taste of that laidback world. The free-ski coach already told us, 'Friends, fun, and fitness. If kids aren't in a group with their friends, tell us and we'll move them. That's what it's all about.' Just imagine a hockey league like that — less serious coaches, friendlier play, a focus on fun. Right." She laughs. "So it looks like no more hockey for our guy. We're letting him decide." Sharon concludes in her typical firm tone.

It's the only way to do it — let the child-athlete decide — but I'm disappointed. I'll miss Sharon. Someone else will need to take on her role, reminding us that we've become involved in this sport *only* so the kids will have fun now and learn an activity they can enjoy for the rest of their lives. The best lessons we take from hockey have nothing to do with winning. Someone else will need to do Sharon's work of making sure common sense has a voice.

• • •

The game ends 10–8 for Fernie. They beat the team that wins the tournament, and in Ollie's math this single victory means his team won the tournament and won the whole season. I let him have his own math. For him, hockey is all about the story, and this game makes a perfect ending.

When the coaches let the parents into the change room, we find a celebration worthy of the Stanley Cup Final. The kids have the music pumped and their shirts off. They dance and yell. We cover our ears but can't help laughing.

When Ollie finally takes a seat for me to undo his skate laces, I pose the question. "So that's it for this season. What do you think — hockey again next year?"

"*Hell yeah!*" he yells loud over the music.

"Ollie! Language!"

"What?" He looks genuinely confused, and then he lowers his voice to a whisper. "Is hell a swear word?"

"Yes, I mean, I think so. But maybe not the worst swear word ever spoken in a hockey locker room."

I pat him on his sweaty head. Atom Year Two has drawn to a close, and *hell yeah* we'll be back next fall. In Pee Wee, mothers will not be allowed in the change room. I don't know it in the moment, but I have unlaced my last pair of hockey skates.

ANOTHER SEASON

The week before we leave on our annual family vacation to Mexico, Marty and I have a fight that feels like the end.

Paul and Julie, old Olympic wrestling friends from Calgary, have come to town for the weekend. Marty's mom agrees to take the kids for the evening, and we are free to double date at a trendy Latin tapas place. But first, a long waitlist forces us next door to a pub. We drink too much beer before even getting a dinner table. When we move to the restaurant, we switch to tequila. Paul and Julie are enjoying some rare kid-free time as well, and we get excessive. Inhibitions vacate the building, and Paul, ignoring Julie's kicks below the table, tells stories about a man I spent some time with in Australia when we were all there for the 2000 Olympics, *nearly twenty years ago*. Marty's mood changes, for the worse. Maybe it's the tequila. Maybe it's a full winter devoting no attention to each other. Or maybe Marty has intuited something of me being pulled elsewhere over the last few months, even if he's remained willfully oblivious to the details. His misplaced jealousy, teetering into hostility, sets the tone for the rest of the evening.

After dinner, we stumble into the street to hear a band playing in the town square. Our late dinner has us off schedule, and the music has already wound down, but Marty and Paul think they might be able to grab a plastic cup of draught beer before last call. I spot a friend and stop to chat while the other three push on to the beer garden. I lose them in the crowd. When I finish my conversation, I'm a little hurt that Marty didn't slow to wait or tell me where to meet him. I make a brief, weak effort to find them. *Fine. He ditched me.* That's how my thinking goes. We live a mere five-minute walk from the stage. So I start home, knowing he'll catch me eventually.

When he gets home thirty minutes later, he's angry. *"You just left us?"*

Our fight escalates and takes us to an ugly place. We've visited that ugliness before, with concerning frequency since we've had kids and more regularly than ever this last year. The mean-spirited hatefulness and end-times emotion does not need to be recreated on the page.

I spend the next day wondering: what did we fight about? I mean: what were we *really* fighting about? Surely all that cruelty and yelling wasn't really about me leaving a beer garden at the end of the night when I'd already had too much to drink. Surely the anger wasn't really about me walking straight home, five minutes away, where I knew Marty would find me. Nor could the nastiness truly have been about Marty going to get a beer instead of hanging at my side while I finished a conversation that he didn't care to join. So what *was* the fight about?

It comes to me late that night when the fog of hangover lifts: we fought about who's in and who's out. Who's sticking with the marriage and who's already abandoned it? Did I leave him at the beer garden? Or did he leave me when he walked off to get beer tickets? *Fear of abandonment. Anger at being uncared for. Pain at being treated as disposable.* Here we have a plausible, understandable source of anger: who left whom?

You can't park a marriage, that's what I realize, not for a whole hockey season, not year after year. This marriage needs some heavy-duty maintenance.

In that frame of mind, we board WestJet to Puerto Vallarta and then on to a little fishing village where my parents spend their winters. They've rented us a one-bedroom bungalow right around the corner from the little pool house where they live from November until April. For the last few years, I've taken the kids to visit my parents alone, a week of sun to break up the mountain winter. This time the four of us go together.

We have a three-hour drive to the Calgary airport, followed by a five-hour flight to Puerto Vallarta. Once we land, we still have a three-hour curvy drive to the village. We all slump in the uncomfortable, sticky-hot van, worn out by the long day of travel. All except Ollie. He's giddy with excitement. He babbles to Pedro, the driver, speaking so fast that I'm not sure Pedro follows.

"I play hockey. It's my favorite sport. Have you ever played hockey? Probably not. You guys don't even have winter. It's cold. It's really hot here. Phew! I'm sweating." Ollie yanks on his long-sleeved red shirt from the Kimberley tournament. It reads *Hockey: Keeping the tooth fairy in business since 1875.* "What do you guys think of Trump, Pedro?" Ollie says it *Trumpf.* "Are you going to build his wall? I don't think you should. Because, like, why should *you* build *his* wall? He's the one who wants it. Why would *you* build it? And why should there even *be* a wall? I think it's stupid. I play center. We won our last game ten to eight against Kimberley and they won the whole tournament, so it's kind of like *we* won the whole tournament. I mean sort of. Depending how you figure it out. Like they're the best team but we beat them so that makes us the best team. And I hope Trumpf doesn't start World War III and I don't even understand why he's president and . . . it's hot here. Do you find it hot here? Have you ever seen snow?"

Poor Pedro. Marty and I catch eyes and share a laugh. In Mexico, our marital weather changes. Marty has always been better at stepping away from an argument. He can start over like other people flick on a light switch. We'll go to bed angry and miserable, and in the morning he'll smile at me in the kitchen, pure lightness. "Good morning, sweetheart!"

When we arrive in the hot sun, he seems happy. More importantly he seems to like *me*. I like being liked.

Marty enjoys small-town Mexican life much more than he ever enjoyed the fancy resorts we've tried. He settles into a simple, joyful routine forging relationships with the villagers despite the language barrier. In the morning, he and Katie mosey off to a little bakery down the street. He uses an iPhone app to piece together enough Spanish to chat with the old ladies. The women must appreciate his effort — or maybe they're drawn to Katie, whose fair skin and red hair stand out in this country. The women scurry Marty and Katie behind the sales counter and into the kitchen, letting them pick from the morning's offerings, still warm from the oven. Cinnamon buns and sugar pastries and pie crust full of yellow custard, all gigantic, for less than fifty cents each. Ollie and I, who haven't budged from our poolside stacks of books, receive the treats gratefully. After a couple of strong coffees and a truckload of sugar, Marty wanders down to the dock and buys fish off the boats, the men just pulling into shore with their morning catch. Marty borrows a Crock-Pot from my parents and spends the rest of the morning chopping and mixing and creating some magical fish stew. Then the four of us walk to the beach with my parents. Ollie and Marty can play in the water for hours, every day, their heads bobbing in the distant waves, me worrying about the strong undertow. They never tire. My skin prunes up just watching them.

Katie takes an interest in surfing, so we get her some lessons. We're astonished at how quickly she learns to stand. On the third try, she rides the wave all the way into shore, her posture rigid and determined. As athletes, she and Ollie are opposites. Katie puts on a competitive glare and listens to instructions with absolute seriousness. She practices a movement over and over until she gets it.

My swim coach Glen Belfry used to define athleticism that way: someone who can take verbal instruction and turn it into physical body movements is an athlete. It's about bodily intelligence.

But in my experience there are different kinds of athletes. Ollie doesn't have the same tendency as Katie to listen with high seriousness or to apply himself to mastering a movement with such focus and precision. He does things his own weird, passionate way. Whatever he does, he does for joy or some other intrinsic, emotional motivation that only Ollie understands. But he does flounder his way into competence (or even excellence) eventually. Compared to Katie, he's equally strong at swimming and surfing, but he's come at those skills in a more intuitive way. He will never commit to an hour-long surfing lesson, but he'll play in the waves on his own for an entire day, and then for an entire week. He will learn by feel.

I wonder if my brother, the wrestling coach, would define athleticism the same as my swim coach did. Over dinner in Mexico, Justin holds up his big fighter's hands and tells us he tried to learn to play guitar after he retired from competition following the 2000 Olympics. "The instructor dude would make his rounds while we all played, stopping by each person with technique tips. At me, he'd just say, 'That's it! You're getting it! Keep it up!' Finally, I said, 'Don't give me that shit. I invented that line. You're getting it? I'm not getting it. I could keep this up for ten years and I wouldn't get it.'" Justin flexes his strong fingers as proof. He has wrestler's hands, not guitarist's hands. He's made the most of those wrestler hands. "'Yeah, you're right,' the guy says to me, 'you're probably never going to get it.'"

An extremely successful athlete, Justin couldn't take the music instructor's verbal cues and translate them into physical movement. He couldn't intuit his way there either. His particular body simply could not do those tasks

I'm curious to see what sport has in store for our kids with their bodies' particular strengths and limitations, their different styles of learning and different ways of applying themselves, their different degrees of coach-ability, and their unique passions. I now see their sporting lives as a series of stories waiting to unfold. I am excited to watch them both.

• • •

I remember being in Mexico last year, when Ollie took to the surf like the son of Poseidon he imagined himself to be. On that holiday, I grabbed on to his enthusiasm for this new sport as a chance to pose the hockey question: should we or shouldn't we?

I ask him again this year, eager to hear his answer after the euphoria of that final win has worn off, but this time I have less optimism that his answer will relieve me of my hockey-mom duties. "So, what do you think, Ollie? You're still liking hockey? You're going to do it next year? Head into Pee Wee?"

"Ahhh . . . *yeah*." He doesn't say *duh*, but I hear it. "Hockey is my favorite sport."

"How come?"

"Well." He shrugs, as awkward as if I've asked him to defend his affection for his favorite grade-four girl. "I like hockey because it's rough. And a team sport. I like team sports. Learning to pass to other people and stuff."

Essentially, he gives the same answer as before. *I like hockey because it's hockey. I like it because I like it.*

We've barely finished this season, and already I see the start of next year's hockey politics driven by parents' egos. It looks like Pee Wee will not have enough kids for two Fernie teams but too many players to work well on one team. Plus, there's no Pee Wee goalie. The only solution offered so far is to have a Bantam goalie play down. That can happen, but it would restrict the team to playing house league instead of rep. Bub has said he won't coach unless there's a rep team, and he won't coach unless there's a good goalie. The response of the parents I have come to respect? *Okay. Goodbye, Bub.*

Why would any parent-coach issue such ultimatums? Is it because he wants to create a good hockey experience for the kids enthusiastic about the sport? Or is it because he wants to feed his own ego by being involved with a winning team?

Parents who choose to be vigilant about their children's participation in sport will have to keep calling out these more sinister elements of hockey culture. The bullying and elitism and mistreatment of players all have a long tradition and a tight hold.

Coach Bub is "old-school." I hear it over and over again — from dads and moms and hockey coaches and hockey administrators, as if "old-school" is the only explanation we need. Well, we're new school. Change is hard, but it's time. I will support Ollie in his desire to play hockey. I will not relinquish him to hockey's culture.

• • •

But we're in Mexico. We're taking a break from hockey. Marty reminds me more than once. "Let's not talk about that," he says, gesturing at the sea and sand and sun.

Each night, after a full day of playing hard in the hot sun, the kids fall asleep easily and quickly. After dinner with my extended family, Marty and I sit on our little patio and talk. I sip on a tequila. Marty drinks beer. Mostly, we talk about how lucky we are to have such happy, healthy, and fun-loving kids. We talk about what interesting human beings they're becoming. We share stories about them and we laugh together until my face hurts. I remember how funny Marty can be.

On holidays, I can see what I forget in our regular life: I like Marty. I like him a lot.

But Marty and I have been together nearly twenty years, and we don't have the fresh excitement of a new relationship anymore. Admitting this comes as a relief. The resentment floats away. The relationship's evolution becomes matter-of-fact instead of a reason to inflict blame. Acknowledging and letting go of what we don't have allows us a new space to voice and appreciate what we do have: a twenty-year friendship, two wonderful kids, respect and admiration for each other's parenting styles, a shared sense of humor. We also holiday together well. We have trouble with the day-to-day life. Neither of us excels at teamwork. Stress exacerbates this challenge. But we always — and still — have fun when we take a break from the work and the stress.

• • •

It turns out Marty has suspected my wandering attention. In this relaxed and satiated state, we talk easily. "Is there someone I should know about?" he asks on the patio once the kids have gone to bed. He speaks tentatively but holds my eyes, and I know he's ready to hear whatever I have to say.

"No," I say, quietly. "There was, but that's done."

"I see."

I tell him a little bit about my online flirtation. It feels good to be honest. Putting my infatuation into words releases some of its power.

"Not someone better than you," I assure Marty. "Someone different. Someone I could talk with about books and writing. Someone interested in my stories you find boring. Someone who seemed to find me exciting instead of demanding. I liked the way he looked at me, the way he listened."

"Because it was new." Marty's matter-of-fact tone surprises me.

"Yes, because it was new."

"And you didn't have to argue about kids' schedules and mortgages and household chores."

"Yes, that too."

Now that I'm having this discussion with my husband, I realize that Marty and Thomas resemble each other, both tall and broad-shouldered with long faces and striking eye color, Marty mossy green, Thomas brown like espresso. Both also have a hint of trouble about them. Or Marty did. The socially sanctioned relationship of marriage bleaches that kind of trouble, and along with it a bit of the danger I find so attractive.

"So why's the flirtation over?"

"His wife."

"Oh."

I wonder if I should tell him more, but he seems to have heard enough. Instead, I say simply, "I love you."

"I know."

"I just liked the idea that I'm not completely done with romance, with excitement, with new affections. I liked the idea that there's a way to continue having those connections with people, the kind of connections that make me feel young and alive, and to explore those connections, without jeopardizing our home life. You and I have been friends for a long time too. I don't want to lose that, ever. But I miss feeling attractive, and I miss getting to know someone in that physically charged way. I miss the excitement."

"I get it. I do." He leans in and kisses me, first on my cheek, then on my ear, and then on my lips. He doesn't do this at home, take time to kiss me. Nor I him. It's good. Still, even in this moment, I can't sink in and fully enjoy his affection or his

219

attentive and open listening. Even in this moment, I'm looking forward, puzzling out how to bring the holiday home.

"I was going to try to talk you into an open relationship," I laugh. "But even on the worst days, I knew: bad idea! On the relationship spectrum, *open* comes right before *over*, not just alphabetically."

"Yes." Marty shakes his head at me in a way that feels like home. He puts up with a lot. I'm grateful he keeps his sense of humor. "Having *more* people to please will not solve our problems."

"I know. We're going to find our way back to each other. That's how we solve our problems."

Over our ten Mexican days, we come in and out of this conversation about our relationship, but in a leisurely and comfortable way. Neither of us seems threatened by the new uncertainty and instability. Maybe we're both relieved to finally say it aloud: something needs to change. We've done the script. We've done love, marriage, baby carriage straight through to hockey rink, ski hill, swimming pool, and we both feel empty. Our kids thrive. Our marriage does not. We need to think about what our happiness might look like beyond that script.

• • •

The last day, we're both lying on the sand, reveling in the late afternoon sun on our bare skin and sipping from frosty beer bottles, when Marty asks, "So this guy . . . Mr. Smarty Pants . . . professor dude . . ." I can see his mind working, but unlike me Marty does not think aloud. I let him take his time. I'm in no rush to go anywhere. This right-now moment is good, the quiet, his hand on my thigh, the hot sun.

"Did you cheat?"

It's a direct question. I get the impression he's ready to hear, no matter the answer.

This time I too am unusually slow with my words. I don't know how to explain, even to myself, the intensity of my feelings for Thomas, the extent to which thoughts of him took over my life for that brief time. My old friend from far away has an answer. "When you swam, did you keep your ribbons?" That's what she asked me. I didn't. I never do. "Men are like that for you," she said. "Once you win them, you discard them. Just like you discarded your ribbons. You can't get rid of Thomas because you didn't get to the podium. It's all about the contest for you, and with Thomas you can't figure out if you won."

It's not a flattering portrait, but I recognize the truth in it. I do like the contest part. I've made everything, even my personal relationships, about winning and losing. My world view has become warped by this insatiable craving for external validation, a desire ingrained in me from my earliest experiences of competitive sport.

Marty waits for his answer.

"Esther Perel . . . she's this psychotherapist and relationship expert . . . you can see her on the internet, on YouTube, on TED Talks. Perel says cheating involves a combination of three things: emotional attachment, physical chemistry, and secrecy." I'm forever a graduate student. I can't resist citing my sources. "Perel says an imagined kiss can be more powerful — and more distracting and disruptive — than a real kiss. By Perel's definition, yes, I cheated."

Marty nods. One quick movement. He says nothing. It's a gesture I know well from Ollie. *Okay. Got it. Moving on.* Marty's not a word guy — he uses few and takes his time with them. He'll have more to say over the next days and weeks and months as he processes this information, on his own schedule and in his own way.

For now, he throws his long sunbathed leg over mine and slides closer until our hips touch. We luxuriate in the golden sun. He scoops me into him, kissing the spot where my shoulder meets my neck.

"Well!" Ollie has appeared, talking down to us. "I'm glad to see you two getting along so well!" Sounding like a fifty-year-old marriage counselor rather than our own little boy, Ollie leans over next to Marty to pick up his surfboard from the sand. We watch him stride toward the ocean. Not that long ago, he waddled, a chubby toddler. Already he's a little man.

Never one to resist the ocean, Marty soon follows. Katie plays UNO with her grandma up in the shade. I'm alone with my thoughts.

As with marriage, I commit to another year of hockey without knowing what it entails. I can't imagine the obstacles the following year will throw in our path. I don't yet know that early in the season the Fernie rink will spring an ammonia leak, killing three men. In the wake of that tragedy, the loss of our arena will seem like a minor inconvenience. Our opponents in Elkford will offer to let the Fernie teams use half of their ice surface for practices. That puts an hour of icy mountain highway between Ollie and each training session — enough to give us pause. Each time we will ask: Does Ollie really want to go? Is it worth it? Should a grade-five boy be arriving home from hockey after ten on a school night?

The pause proves useful. I strive to implement that same breathing room into other areas of our life.

With that extra breath, we lighten up on the hockey front. Ollie goes to the practices when he wants and when the schedule works. This change forces us to admit what has always been true, what is true for most North American families: our involvement in hockey is purely recreational.

We begin to act accordingly. If the commute to a game or tournament feels too onerous, we skip. I let up a little on my determination to use sport as a vehicle to teach my kids commitment and discipline. In the space, other lessons will grow, lessons like the value of moderation and the importance of family time. I get a ski pass for the first time since hockey became demanding. We enjoy full family ski days, but the pass also means I can get up to the hill to watch Katie race. In this new year, I will no longer be so fully absorbed in supporting one child that I have no time for the other two members of my family.

But not all of the year's changes will be about doing less. To all my projects, I will add a new one: making my husband happy. I will be surprised to discover how much joy that endeavor brings me and how enthusiastically he reciprocates. I might say that in this year to come our whole family wins, except that I'm working hard to unlearn my tendency to evaluate life in terms of winning and losing.

Right now, though, on this beach in the salty air, I don't know what the coming year will bring. I dig my toes into the warm sand and hold my cold beer bottle against my cheek. I watch Marty and Ollie ride the Mexican surf. Each time a wave brings them to shore, they paddle farther into the deep water. The sun falls to a low angle, glaring off the water. The few humans left in the ocean become shadows. I see Marty and Ollie together, then they seem to drift apart, then I lose them. I think of the strong undertow. Only two days ago, it pulled my five-year-old nephew out above his head. Katie tried to help get him back, but soon she too was in tears. My sister-in-law and I noticed and were sprinting down to their aid when a tourist fished them both out, dragging them up to the beach with judgmental stares at us negligent parents.

But Ollie is bigger and stronger. He knows how to handle the current. I think. But where is he? I hold my hand to block the sun. I make out Marty's long body, straddling a surfboard far out in the flat water. But where's Ollie? I scan the waves. I can't see Ollie's slick brown hair, his sturdy little shoulders. I know I have a tendency to overreact. I imagine Marty shaking his head at me, laughing at my panic, and I try to assure myself all is well: Marty's out there with Ollie — what could go wrong?

But I can see Marty, I think, and I can't see Ollie. I count backwards from ten as my eyes dart from swimming shadow to swimming shadow.

Ollie is strong in the water. He knows the ocean. He can hold his breath a long time. He's got his dad out there.

He's probably playing down along the ocean floor. I squint into the glare of the setting sun. I can't see anything.

I need a glimpse of an Ollie-foot or an Ollie-hand. I need to see his Ollie-butt in the air as he dives over a big wave. I need some happy splashing, because really I don't see him anywhere. For sure now I recognize Marty way out on the horizon, waiting for the perfect wave.

No Ollie.

I'm on my feet, and I don't like the desperation rising in my chest. I'm being irrational. I know the current is strong, but Ollie doesn't take risks. He's my safe kid. He'd swim straight for shore if he felt the ocean's pull.

"Ollie!" I hear the frantic note of alarm in my voice, but I yell again. "*OLLIE!*"

And then I see him, his sleek seal head pops up, his brown strong back curving across the arc of a wave. When the ocean spits him out, he looks my way, his face golden in the sun. He waves, his smile huge.

My hand is on my heart. *Thank you, thank you, thank you.* I say it aloud though I don't know who I'm thanking.

I glance up the beach to see fair Katie still playing Uno in the shade. She throws her head back, her mouth wide in laughter. Probably, she's cheated Grandma out of victory, again.

In this moment, I recognize my main job as a mother: standing guard for my children's safety and well-being and otherwise getting out of the way to let Ollie and Katie be Ollie and Katie. I wave out into the ocean and blow a kiss. He's okay. He's happy. But I don't return to the dry beach. I'll stand here, knee-deep in the ocean, my gaze tight on my son.

ACKNOWLEDGMENTS

THANKS . . .

To Katie and Ollie — for all they teach me, all they make me see anew, all they ways they inspire.

To Marty — for Ollie and Katie, and for always learning with me how to do this life thing better. I love you and your kooky chickpea-peeling ways. XOXO IRL.

To Frank and Johnna Abdou — for . . . where do I start? For everything.

To Justin Abdou — for being the little brother I've always looked up to. Also thanks for the early reading to make sure I didn't say anything stupid about sports. (Phew!)

To all my fellow hockey moms and dads — for the camaraderie.

To Jesse Finkelstein and Sam Haywood — for being my all-star agent team! You two astound, always.

To Susan Renouf — for early enthusiasm and continual editorial insights. From our first phone conversation, I knew you were the editor for this book. I was right. And to Laura Pastore and Susannah Ames and the rest of the ECW team for bringing this book into the world and helping it find its readers.

To the Sport Literature Association crew — for being my first audience.

To Steven Heighton — for complimenting me on my work ethic often enough that I feel compelled to try to live up to your idea of me.

To my colleagues at Athabasca University — for the collegiality.

To Trevor Dumba — for *Have fun! Try hard!* and other words to live by.

To Lauren B. Davis — for mentorship and friendship, and for being a first reader again.

To Ginger Pharand, Gyllian Phillips, Andy Sinclair, Hal Wake, Anna Sam Hudson, Patricia Westerhof, John Vaillant, Keith Liggett, Trevor Cole, Randall Maggs, Janice MacDonald, Randy Williams, Lorna Crozier, Sioux Browning, Ayelet Tsabari, Gordon Sombrowski, and Kevin Allen — for stimulating conversation and reliable friendship.

To Christian Bök — for being one of the first writers to whom, in a dark prairie bar over a cold pint of beer, I confessed the earliest hints of this book. Thank you for not saying "What a stupid idea!" That one sentence, from you, would have ended this book before it had begun.

To Kevin Patterson — for early readings, for friendship, and for generously sharing the sailboat on which the earliest draft of this book was written. ·

To Harley Rustad — who traveled a parallel journey with his

own manuscript at the same time and kept me company (never underestimate the power of a spirited word-count competition).

To my Soar Cycle sisters (& brother!) — again for the sweat-induced sanity.

To memoirists who inspired — Ian Brown (*Sixty*), Jowita Bydlowska (*Drunk Mom*), Camilla Gibb (*This Is Happy*), and Alison Pick (*Between Gods*).

SELECTED READING LIST

Alexander, Kate, Anne Stafford, and Ruth Lewis. *The Experiences of Children Participating in Organised Sport in the UK.* The University of Edinburgh/NSPCC. Child Protection Research Centre. October 2011.

Bidini, Dave. *Keon and Me: My Search for the Lost Soul of the Leafs.* Toronto: Penguin, 2014.

Campbell, Ken, and Jim Parcels. *Selling the Dream: How Hockey Parents and their Kids Are Paying the Price for Our National Obsession.* Penguin: Toronto, 2014.

Code, David. *To Raise Happy Kids, Put Your Marriage First.* The Crossroad Publishing Company: New York, 2009.

Dryden, Ken. *Game Change: The Life and Death of Steve Montador, and the Future of Hockey.* Signal: Toronto, 2017.

Dvorak, Petula. "Our Ten Year Old Decided to Give Hockey a Try. What We Encountered Was Dreadful." *The Washington Post.* October 5, 2015.

Feiler, Bruce. *The Secrets of Happy Families.* William Morrow Paperbacks: New York, 2013.

Fleury, Theo. *Playing with Fire.* HarperCollins: Toronto, 2010.

Frank, Megan. *Choosing to Grow for the Sport of It: Because All Kids Matter.* justforthesportofit.wordpress.com

Fraser, Jennifer Margaret. *Teaching Bullies: Zero Tolerance in the Court or in the Classroom.* Motion Press, 2015.

Gaston, Bill. *Midnight Hockey: All about Beers, Boys, and the Real Canadian Game.* Anchor Canada: Toronto, 2007.

Gladwell, Malcolm. *Outliers: The Story of Success.* Back Bay Books: New York, 2011.

Judd, Wes. "Why the Ice Is White." *The Pacific Standard.* June 19, 2015.

Johnson, Matthew D. *Great Myths of Intimate Relationships: Dating, Sex, and Marriage.* Wiley-Blackwell: Hoboken, New Jersey, 2016.

Laraque, Georges. *Georges Laraque: The Story of NHL's Unlikeliest Tough Guy.* Viking: Toronto, 2011.

Laumann, Silken. *Child's Play: Rediscovering the Joy of Play in Our Families and Communities.* Vintage Canada: Toronto, 2007.

Lawrence, Grant. *The Lonely End of the Rink: Confessions of a Reluctant Hockey Goalie.* Vancouver: Douglas & MacIntyre, 2013.

Levine, Madeline. *The Price of Privilege: How Parental Pressure and Material Advantage Are Creating a Generation of Disconnected and Unhappy Kids.* HarperCollins: New York, 2008.

Omalu, Bennet. *Truth Doesn't Have a Side: My Alarming Discovery about the Danger of Contact Sports.* Zondervan Publishing: Michigan, 2017.

O'Sullivan, John. *Changing the Game: The Parents Guide to Raising Happy, High Performing Athletes and Giving Youth Sports Back to Our Kids.* Morgan James Publishing: New York, 2013.

Perel, Esther. *The State of Affairs: Rethinking Infidelity.* Harper: New York, 2017.

Quarrington, Paul. *King Leary.* Anchor Canada: Toronto, 2007.

Smith, Stephen. *Puckstruck: Distracted, Delighted and Distressed by Canada's Hockey Obsession.* Greystone Books: Vancouver, 2014.

Waldman, Ayelet. *Bad Mother: A Chronicle of Maternal Crimes, Minor Calamities, and Occasional Moments of Grace.* Anchor: New York, 2010.

Woods, Judith. "Not on the Team? Then No More Sport for You." *The Telegraph.* January 2015.

Wulf, Steve. "The Grand Total of Youth Hockey." ESPN. July 2, 2013.

© Kevan Wilkie

Angie Abdou is the author of five novels, including, most recently, *In Case I Go*, a finalist in the fiction category of the Banff Mountain Book Award and named one of 2017's most riveting mysteries by *Chatelaine* magazine. *The Bone Cage* was a CBC Canada Reads finalist, defended by NHL star Georges Laraque, and was awarded the 2011–12 MacEwan Book of the Year. Angie is an associate professor of creative writing at Athabasca University.

At ECW Press, we want you to enjoy this book in whatever format you like, whenever you like. Leave your print book at home and take the eBook to go! Purchase the print edition and receive the eBook free. Just send an email to ebook@ecwpress.com and include:

Get the eBook free!*
*proof of purchase required

- the book title
- the name of the store where you purchased it
- your receipt number
- your preference of file type: PDF or ePub

A real person will respond to your email with your eBook attached. And thanks for supporting an independently owned Canadian publisher with your purchase!